The Whitechapel Fog

A Novel
By
Michael Generali

Printed in the United States of America

First Printing: 2011

ISBN: 0615539661

EAN-13: 978-0615539669

Author's Disclaimer: This book, while based on certain historical facts, is a work of fiction. Some names may have been changed, and some of the events and characters may have been fictionalized for dramatic purposes. Names, characters, places, and incidents are either the product of the author's imagination or are based on historical facts, but used fictitiously. Any resemblance to actual persons, living or dead, or business establishments, or locales is entirely coincidental, except for those historical matters that are commonly known or are part of the public record.

Also by Michael Generali:

Seasons…of Fantasies and Dreams
(ISBN: 1453622128)
(EAN-13 9781453622124)

Acknowledgement

No book can be written without the help, understanding and support from family, friends and business associates. I thank everyone for his or her contribution, no matter how big or small that may have been.

The Whitechapel Fog

Prologue

"In London there is an East End and a West End. In the West End are those fortunate ones who are sent into the world with a kiss. In the East End are the others. Here live the poor, the shamed. Those who's fate, seeing how shrunken and bent they are as they creep through the gates of life are spat in their face for good measure. In this East End a corner has been set aside where, not content with the spittle, fate sends the poor on their way with a blow, a kick and their hats pulled over their eyes. In this spot, with the holy name of Whitechapel, we would have to sink or swim, survive or go under, find bread, or if we could not, find death."

- Jacob Adler (1888)

I.

Even the mosquito, that menacing insect with the penetrating needle, refused to fly when the blue fog arrived in the evening. Most people, however, took little notice of the misty shroud, except for considering it another nuisance in the cold, damp and wet London weather. For centuries, the blue fog prevailed in Europe. It often all but disappeared for decades at a time, only to reappear when that which lived within it was revived.

One night a gentle wisp of the barely noticeable bluish-hued fog appeared, softly floating through the poorer, overcrowded quarters of the city known as the East End. It then dissipated with the morning sun, only to reappear the following night. With each appearance, the fog became slightly thicker, bluer and more noticeable. People looking out upon the Thames could watch it hover above the river. Never touching the water, it moved northward toward the shore and the Whitechapel district that it seemed to favor. One might have thought that it was being driven by the current in the river or by a slow breeze. However, careful scrutiny, had there been any, would have revealed that the water flowed eastward towards the sea, and the air was still while the fog moved. Yet, it appeared to harbor no malice. To the few who did observe it, it was simply the fog. The blue fog hung in the air. It watched; it waited.

***

The final day of August saw an early morning murder near Essex Wharf on Buck's Row. It was a drunken, middle-aged woman whose throat had been cut and lower abdomen viciously sliced open. The ensuing investigation left the police baffled and without any suspect. London was about to enter a period of uncertainty that would drive an escalating level of fear throughout the populace.

The early morning light pushed the blackness of night away, and with it, the fog dissipated once more. Still, no one took more than a casual notice of this event. News of the murder had not yet spread through the dank streets and dirty alleys of the over-populated East End. The people began their new day of existence the same as they had the day before, in a repetitive routine of subsistence living.

II.

William Johnstone, a retired colonel from Queen Victoria's India Expeditionary Force, was included in the group of people who took little notice of the latest happenings in the night. His service record had been exemplary, and he had been involved in some of the fiercest fighting that the force had seen. To his benefit, this resulted in a quick rise through the ranks. He received several wounds during the last campaign in which he was involved. Following his recovery, which lasted an entire year, he requested, and was granted, an early discharge from the Queen's Service. At Johnstone's request his aide-de-camp, James Potter, a good soldier in his own right, was permitted to leave as well to continue his position with the colonel.

Now in his late forties, Johnstone returned to his mother country, which he had not seen in a quarter of a century. The restlessness and uncertainty of army life now left behind, and the lack of living relatives, all brought forth a pining for a more stable environment. Johnstone wanted close access to London without living within its walls, and he wanted a tranquil location where intrusion from other people would be at a minimum. To that end, he and Potter scouted a several acre plot of land along England's signature river between London and Thurrock. Built thereupon was a small, but comfortable four-room cottage of stone with a thatched roof. The driveway from the main road was lined with shrubbery. It led to the main door of the cottage, and continued to a small, stone carriage house and wooden barn that were not too distant from the house. Potter had taken an interest in flower gardening, and maintained a floral display that encircled the cottage. He cultivated different sets of flowers that were specific for each season, except winter.

Johnstone's old, never broken, army habit of rising early brought him from his bed before sunrise. As he washed and groomed himself for the coming day's activities, his long-time and fiercely loyal aide sorted the clothing that Johnstone would wear that day. From his long tenure of service with the colonel, Potter had also developed the habit of rising early.

With the task completed, Potter removed himself to the kitchen, and began preparing their breakfast. The room was small with shelving and a pantry hung on the wall, and a stove, sink and counter for preparing meals. A small, square table with four chairs occupied most of the remaining area in the room.

Now that he was retired, Johnstone did not demand or desire much protocol regarding his rank. He tolerated being called "Colonel" and "Sir" mostly because he could not get his army associates to address him in non-military terms. However, over time, he was able to get Potter to drop the titles, for the most part. Generally, he preferred to take care of himself, and this morning was standing in front of the large mirror in his bedroom. He was putting the finishing touches on his attire when his keen sense of smell alerted him that his breakfast was ready. He deeply breathed in the aroma of baking biscuits accompanied with fried eggs and ham.

He left the modest-sized bedroom, which was on the opposite

end of the cottage from the kitchen, walking through the larger front room and on to the location where his senses told him that his appetite would be satisfied.

"Good morning, Colonel!" greeted Potter upon seeing him enter the kitchen.

"Good morning," Johnstone rolled his eyes upward and slightly shook his head at Potter's using military rank to greet him.

"Breakfast is all prepared. Have a seat at the table and I'll bring it to you!"

"Thank you."

The aide went over to the cooking area to prepare two plates. While he did so, Johnstone sat in his usual chair located on the side of the table that permitted him to look out into the front room rather than having his back turned towards it. This was another habit learned in the army that he had not broken.

Johnstone had always lived a modest life, and was not overly concerned with the trappings of his rank and former profession. He desired little more than what the small cottage provided. He preferred the solitude that offered the chance to forget the many battles. If they needed anything, he or Potter would venture into Thurrock or London, but those were infrequent journeys.

Potter placed the plates on the table. "Here you are!"

Johnstone took a deep breath. "The food smells exceptionally good this morning. Well done!"

"Maybe you are just exceptionally hungry this morning!"

"Nonsense! I have never had the occasion to criticize any meal that you have prepared for me!"

"I appreciate the kind remark," acknowledged Potter as he sat down at the table across from Johnstone, "however, I seem to recall one night in a cave near Jammu…"

Johnstone frowned as the memory came to him. "Oh yes. I forgot about that. Those rats were certainly not delicious."

They both laughed and began to eat their breakfast.

Their former professional relationship had turned into one of comradeship. Johnstone tried to treat Potter as one with equal standing. Still, protocol demanded that Potter respect Johnstone's position. Despite this, Johnstone often helped and shared in the chores. Since Potter did receive a stipend for his work, however, he was responsible for the household duties regardless of how much Johnstone assisted with the various tasks.

Breakfast was usually a quiet event. Johnstone preferred to contemplate his activities for the day. It also afforded him the opportunity to awaken fully, lingering sleepiness being one of the consequences of rising out of bed so early in the morning. Potter also appreciated the few moments of quiet that breakfast normally offered.

"Very good, if I may say so again," remarked Johnstone as he finished and patted his stomach with his hands.

"Yes, I agree. I woke up this morning and just had a taste for some ham."

Johnstone smiled slyly, "I'll have a go with the pots and pans tomorrow to see if I can better your culinary performance from this morning!"

"Give it a try. We shall see how it turns out!"

Potter knew that Johnstone's aptitude in the kitchen was on the low side. His cooking efforts were usually edible, but lacking in many respects. In addition, when he was finished, the kitchen looked more like a war zone than part of a home.

They both rose from the table. Potter began the cleanup while Johnstone started for the front room.

"Did you get a chance to check to see if today's Times has arrived?" Johnstone asked the daily after-breakfast question.

Potter's answer was the usual daily response, "Yes. I brought it in and placed it in the front room on your desk."

"Good. I believe I shall enjoy my pipe while I read the paper."

The front room, which was the largest room in the cottage, was furnished with a couch, small table, a couple of chairs and Johnstone's desk and seat. The furniture in the cottage was modest, but appropriate for that type of home. Positioned above the couch hung a banner from Johnstone's India regiment. It was given to him as a gift from his troops when he retired. His battle sword was on the wall above his desk. It was held in place by a couple of strategically placed, but loose, wooden pegs.

The front door and a window in the front room faced south towards the river. The main highway was distanced about one hundred yards from the back of the cottage, and like the river went east to the sea and west to London.

Johnstone sat at the desk and began to prepare his pipe. However, he stopped when he looked down at the newspaper.

"My God!" he exclaimed as he jumped up from the seat, picked up the newspaper and went to the kitchen where Potter was just finishing the cleaning.

"What is it?"

"Did you read this paper before we ate breakfast?"

"I glanced at the first page when I brought it inside, but that was all."

"No, no, no, that's not what I meant. You know I don't mind you reading the paper before I get to it."

"Then what's the matter?"

Johnstone pointed to an article on the first page. "What do you think of this?"

"It's dreadful. That makes three this year."

"And now two this month! All in Whitechapel too, I might add. What the bloody hell is going on there?"

"I wish I knew. Evidently the police haven't much of a clue either."

Johnstone read the article and continued, "Terrible, like it's all falling apart…and did you see this item?"

"Which one?"

"Where a few people reported spotting a blue fog floating from the river into Whitechapel."

"A blue fog?"

"Yes, of all things, a blue fog!" Johnstone snorted. "Most likely the effects of too much gin and ale, I'd wager."

"A blue fog did it say?" Potter questioned again.

"Yes. Why does it seem to interest you so?"

"May I see the paper, please?"

Johnstone handed the paper to him.

Potter read the article. "Hmm, I didn't see that when I brought in the paper. I was focused on the story about the murder."

"Is there any significance to this fog?" asked Johnstone, slightly confused over Potter's reaction to the article.

"I'm not sure. Maybe it's nothing, but it certainly is strange."

"Well, it certainly has gotten your interest…"

Their conversation was interrupted by a knock at the door.

"Do you think that's the postman?" Johnstone asked.

"No. It's too early for him."

Potter went to the front room and opened the door. "Yes, may I help you?" he asked the visitor.

"Thomas!" Johnstone interrupted, as he had followed Potter to the door.

"William! My God, it's good to see you, old chap!"

Potter stood aside to permit the visitor to enter the cottage as the two enthusiastically shook hands at their reunion.

"Sit down! Sit down!" Johnstone invited. He looked at Potter and then said, "Thomas, forgive me. May I introduce James Potter, my aide. Potter, this is Colonel Thomas Morrison."

The two exchanged greetings, and Morrison then sat down on the couch. Johnstone sat in one of the chairs and instructed Potter to make some tea.

"This is certainly unexpected, Thomas," Johnstone began. "I don't get many visitors here. I have come to like my solitude, and sometimes I forget how good it can be to see someone from the past."

"I know what you mean. After all of the campaigns, wars and

battles, a peaceful setting is a nice prize." Morrison turned his head, looked up at the regimental banner hanging on the wall, and identified it. "After we were together in Egypt for many years, you were promoted and sent to India."

"Yes, that's correct. You also were promoted shortly after I left, and remained in Egypt for the rest of your career, right?"

Morrison smiled, "We may have not seen each other for many a year, but it's nice to hear that because of our friendship we kept informed on each other's career and whereabouts!"

"I left the service a couple of years ago. It doesn't seem that long a time yet, but it is."

"I heard you had some difficult times in India."

"We all did; we still do, but it is no longer my fight."

"True," Morrison agreed. "We paid for our retirement by facing death as it tried to defeat us. God, I watched as so many of our friends and the soldiers under our commands were lost. You, my dear chap, were extremely lucky to get out of there alive!"

"Yes," Johnstone spoke solemnly, "Many fine men are not here today, their dreams and ambitions lost forever."

There was a moment of silence as both men reflected on the past.

Potter returned to the room. He was carrying a tray that contained the teapot, cups and a couple of scones. He placed the tray on the small table in front of the couch, and then served the beverage to both men. Their mood returned to a more uplifted state.

"Stay with us, Potter, and pour yourself some tea too, if you like," Johnstone invited.

"Thank you, Sir," Potter replied. When others were present, Potter would revert to the formality and protocol of rank. He poured himself some tea and sat in the vacant chair.

"Colonel Morrison and I go back a long time in our careers with the Queen's Service."

"Yes, indeed we do!"

They both laughed.

"Would you like a pipe, Thomas?" asked Johnstone.

"Most definitely, thank you! Especially if you still obtain that fine tobacco from America. Do you still get it from our former colony?" he chuckled.

"I wait at the dock when the ship comes in!"

"Splendid!"

"Actually, I have a distant cousin who lives there. I visited him once many years ago. He sends me a package of tobacco every now and then."

Johnstone stood and retrieved the pipe stand from his desk. He placed it on the table near the couch. The two men prepared their pipes and lit the tobacco. Potter did not smoke.

"Now Thomas, it has been many years since we've seen each other. What brings you here today?"

"The news is the reason for my visit," he motioned towards the newspaper.

"The news?"

"Yes."

"The news about what?"

"The murders in Whitechapel."

"Oh," Johnstone nodded his head while taking several puffs on his pipe.

"Last night was the second this month, and the third since April."

"I read about the murders in the *Times*. There's something in the paper seemingly every other day about them. I tell you that it appears to me that this is getting a bit too sensationalized. But, surely you didn't intend to make this visit and see me just to talk about three murdered prostitutes."

"You're right. I didn't come here just to talk about that."

"What is it then?"

"William, the police are stumped. They have no idea who is responsible for these killings."

"And your interest in all this is?"

"They have asked me to assist them in the investigation. They need help, desperately. Sure, they find several who make good suspects. The police interrogate them; they interview witnesses. The police even conduct identification parades, but not one has been proven to be the killer! The people living in the East End, God love them, are terrified. Two murders like this in one month are only going to make things much worse!"

"When did you get involved with all this?" Potter asked.

"After the second murder. The police initially thought a soldier committed that one. It was then that a friend of mine, Sir Charles Warren, considered my army background, contacted me, and requested my help."

"Sir Charles Warren, the police commissioner?" Johnstone asked.

"Yes, that's right. I helped investigate the second murder. I was able to help them discern that it was not a soldier who perpetrated that crime."

"At least the name of the service was cleared this time." Johnstone rubbed his chin with his hand and squirmed a little in the chair. A slight smile came onto his face. He pointed a finger at Morrison and said, "Thomas, you're leading me with this discussion, and I know where it's heading!"

"Yes, I suppose it's quite obvious. I need your help, and Potter's too, for that matter."

"I don't know," Johnstone tried to dissuade him.

"It'll be invigorating to do this! The three of us returning to action for Queen and Country!"

The patriotic inducement did not sway Johnstone. He had seen his life spent in the service, and believed that he had earned his rest. He looked over at Potter and could see that his aide was hoping for a positive response from him.

Before Johnstone could reply, Morrison calculated that he needed to add more to complete the enticement. "It won't take long. We'll only be helping the Metropolitan Police and Scotland Yard until the perpetrator is caught. How long could that take, with all the resources of those two organizations at work? In addition, with all the people who live in the East End, I'm sure there are plenty of witnesses that the police haven't talked to. They just haven't been found yet. We need to find them and bring them forward for the police to question. Just a few days are all it should take by my book. So, what do you say, old chap? Shall we have another go at it together?"

Johnstone looked over once again at Potter. "Well, Potter, what do you think?"

"It would be a nice change of pace to get out and do this, Sir."

Johnstone took a deep breath. "I don't know where this is going to lead us, but all right, let's get on with it."

"Splendid!" chimed Morrison. "Are you ready?"

"Ready for what?"

"Ready to begin, of course!"

Potter rose to his feet. Johnstone, seeing no further alternative, also rose and motioned towards the door.

Morrison stood and put his hand on the breast pocket of his jacket. "Oh," he said, as he pulled out an envelope and handed it to Johnstone.

"What's this?" Johnstone asked.

"It's a formal request from Sir Charles asking for your assistance. I told him you'd agree to join me without the need for a formal letter, but he insisted on writing it just in case you needed some additional persuading."

Johnstone smiled and shook his head. "Bother that! You had it all calculated, didn't you?" He walked over to the desk and placed the envelope on it. "Well, let's get a move on so we can help solve this bloody mess!"

III.

They rode together in Morrison's carriage to Scotland Yard, where Johnstone and Potter were introduced to the police commissioner. Sir Charles Warren had retired a general from the army. On his way to that rank, he had mixed successes in the various wars that were fought in British South Africa, including being severely wounded in one campaign. However, during his tenure in the British Royal Engineers, he showed ingenuity that brought him decorations and notoriety, including being the first in the British Army to use observation balloons in the field. After leaving the army, he entered politics and ran for a seat in Parliament. He lost by only a narrow margin. A few weeks later, however, he was appointed police commissioner.

Sir Charles was sharply dressed to fit his position. He was in his early forties and had an energetic, youthful look. He was well groomed and wore a full moustache that gave him an authoritative appearance.

Sir Charles began by giving the men a brief overview of the murders. He then invited them to attend a briefing with the investigators assigned to the cases. The briefing included information on the latest murder that had not yet been released to the newspapers. When the meeting was completed, Morrison took Johnstone and Potter to the scenes of the first two murders. Following that, they visited the scene of the most recent.

"What do you know of this scene, Colonel?" asked Potter.

"Only what we were told in the briefing at Scotland Yard. This is my first time here," Morrison answered.

At the crime scene, they met with the inspectors who had just been assigned the case by Scotland Yard to assist the overwhelmed Metropolitan Police. They discussed the incident and surveyed the area.

When finished, they returned to the carriage and rode into London to Morrison's flat. He was living on the top floor of a three-story apartment house, which was located in a good, but not fashionable neighborhood. Morrison introduced the two men to his spouse of many years, and his two teenage children, a boy and a girl. Morrison's wife invited them to stay for supper, which they accepted.

All three men had made the army their career. Now retired, Johnstone was the youngest, with Potter and Morrison in their early fifties. Only Morrison had ever married.

During the course of the meal, the men continued their discussion of the police investigations. Several times Morrison's wife implored them to change the topic so as not to upset the children. They tried, but they had become totally engrossed in the topic, and the conversation inevitably returned to the murders.

The dinner, which for the others in the room was a nightmare, finally ended. Mrs. Morrison insisted that the men retire to the study if they desired to continue their discussions. The men apologized profusely and did as she requested.

Alone in the study, the three considered various strategies as to how they might best assist the police. Morrison provided everyone with brandy and cigars to help stimulate the conversation.

"We need to investigate Whitechapel at night," Morrison proposed. "That is when all of the murders have taken place, and that will be when most of the people who we need to see are the most active."

"I totally agree," Potter stated.

"Good, then let's head over there."

"Now?" asked a tired Johnstone.

"Best time as any," answered Morrison. "What it looked like during the day is fresh in our minds, but now is the time the troublemakers appear. Everything looks and everyone behaves differently after the sun goes down. It's also Saturday night, and all three murders have taken place on the weekend."

Johnstone was hesitant, "The reality is that there have only been three murders of the type we've been asked to help with in the past five months. I think the odds of us finding anything tonight would be very small indeed."

"Granted, William," acknowledged Morrison, "and I don't think we would catch the suspect unless he ran straight into us. However, we might be able to hear talk in the street, in the pubs, anywhere in the district that might prove pivotal to the investigation."

"You do have a point there," agreed Johnstone. "I suppose that particularly since the latest murder occurred last night, things should be quite fresh in some of the people's minds."

Morrison concurred, "The longer we wait to go to the district, the less we will be able to hear as the people will return to their normal lives and talk of the murders will be pushed aside for other topics."

"All right, then I think we should go there tonight," Johnstone agreed.

"Don't you think we're a little overdressed to be out at night in that area?" asked Potter, referring to the more formal attire that they had donned for their earlier meeting at Scotland Yard.

"Have you ever been in the Whitechapel District before today?"

"I only pass through a small portion of the East End when we travel to London proper," Johnstone replied. "No real need to go inside the district."

"It's the same for me," Potter acknowledged, "but I do get to London more often than Colonel Johnstone." He smiled at his levity.

Johnstone looked at Potter and smirked.

"Well," Morrison spoke, "there are people who go into the district from all social classes, and for all different reasons. Some are for good and others for ill. I'm not casting judgment on the people who live there or those who visit. I'm just making a statement of fact." Morrison then concluded, "Your clothing will be fine."

"All right," Johnstone agreed, "then it's settled and we go tonight. However, I would hate to waste this fine brandy and cigar. I suggest we finish our evening here, and then depart. I also want to thank your lovely wife for the excellent dinner."

IV.

The carriage ride from Colonel Morrison's home took them southwesterly to Whitechapel Road and past London Hospital. The cobblestone-lined street was relatively smooth until they reached Whitechapel High Street, one of the main thoroughfares through Whitechapel.

The East End was comprised of several poverty-laden districts of which Whitechapel was the heart. Like all neighborhoods and districts in any city, some areas were worse than others. Whitechapel, however, was predominantly filled with overcrowded tenements and workhouses. The population was comprised generally of poor immigrants trying to live as best they could given their circumstances and conditions.

Sections of the cobblestone streets were covered in soil, giving the streets the appearance of dirt roads. Puddles of rancid water sat in potholes and along the curbs, giving off a stale urine smell. Feces, from both animal and man, were scattered about and in sufficient quantity that it necessitated one's attention to avoid stepping into the waste. Decaying trash was strewn about in small and large piles. The lowest semblance of humanity would dig through the garbage looking for any edible scrap of food, often fighting off rats, feral cats and roaming dogs. For many people, it would be their sole source of food for the day.

The buildings were plentiful and tightly packed together with narrow, winding streets and dead-end alleys. Many buildings were in disrepair with crumbled bricks and broken windows, but were still inhabited mostly out of necessity, due to the lack of adequate living quarters in the area. There were some stores that plied foods and wares, but in insufficient quantities to meet the demands of the large populace that lived in the district.

Families often numbered four or five in one apartment in the dismal tenement buildings, if they could afford to pay the rent. Others were relegated to living on the streets by day. If they were able to earn a few pence, they could spend the night cramped with dozens in a dosshouse. Those unable to earn even the smallest amount spent the night sleeping in doorways or stairways hoping that they could survive unmolested until morning.

The overpopulated district was unable to breathe and the air hung thick and dank, producing its own sulfurous smog from the factories and railroad that encircled it. The smog was often thick and green in color. The residents referred to it as "pea soup".

There were six taverns and public houses in Whitechapel that were open for twenty hours a day. These establishments attracted everyone in the district, including the children. The lack of sanitary drinking water was replaced with gin, ale and wine. At night, the taverns and pubs were filled with men and women who had nothing to lose and nothing to gain. Outside the establishments, people staggered about as they attempted to advance from one pub to the next. Some who were unable to do so simply lay down on the narrow sidewalks and passed out, often in the doorway of a ramshackle building. Others unable to hold the liquor that controlled them, vomited wherever they stood, adding to the retched waste on the sidewalks and streets. Still others relieved themselves without any shame and in the dark, narrow alleys one could find men and women openly engaged in carnal activities. The more than one thousand prostitutes in the East End worked their pitches and offered themselves for pennies in order to buy drink, a meal or a place to sleep.

The population at night was comprised of more than just those who lived in the district. There were the seamen who had arrived on the ships and walked to the pubs from the nearby docks. There were those who came to the district from the surrounding area looking for the cheap recreation and entertainment that gave Whitechapel its soiled reputation. Those who visited did what they came for, and when they went home, they left the degradation to those who had to suffer through it every day.

The three men left the carriage with Morrison's coachman at an area that they believed would be safe, disembarking and walking north into the heart of the district. As they reached their destination, what they saw was a stark contrast from what they observed during the daytime, and from what they were accustomed to in their own lives. The September night was rank with the odor of summer sweat.

Now and then they were alerted by screams, yelling, drunken fights and police whistles. Crime was rampant in the East End, with murder being a common event in itself.

"Hmm, *Ten Bells*," commented Potter.

"What was that you said?" asked Johnstone.

"I was just reading the name of the pub that we just passed. Has a nautical-related name."

"To lure the sailors, no doubt," Morrison responded.

"Thomas," exclaimed Johnstone, "this scene just goes on from one street and alley to the next. The wretchedness of all this is certainly revolting! My God, this is London, the heart and soul of our empire! Even the conditions in India were better than this! No wonder the police are unable to find their suspect!"

Morrison suggested that they walk down to the docks to clear their heads of what they had seen and find a spot where the noise would be abated enough so they could discuss their plans. The filth and stench stretched to the docks, even extending into the water. However, the volume of people was not as large near the docks, and it was quieter. They walked along the waterfront and their conversation digressed to the past.

"You know, William, I almost joined the navy instead of the army."

"Are you serious, Thomas? I never would have guessed that of you. What changed your mind?"

"I thought that being away at sea would keep me from home for too long a time." Morrison then chuckled and concluded, "I found out that the army took me away even longer!"

"I think you're right about that," Johnstone agreed. "It's easier to keep men assigned to a post longer when they're on land than it is when they're on the water, I think."

"Still, I believe I made the decision that was best for me," Morrison concluded, but not in an altogether convincing manner, and there was a slight hint of disappointment in his voice.

They reached the lock that provided the passageway for ships to and from the Thames.

"Gentlemen, look out on the river," Potter stopped and pointed.

"What is that?" asked Morrison.

They looked out upon a blue fog floating about six feet above the water.

"Have you ever seen anything like this before, William?" asked Morrison.

"Not that I can recall."

"I believe I have," Potter stated.

"Are you sure, Potter?" asked a surprised Johnstone. "Where would you have seen something like this?"

"It was many years ago when I was a courier in Her Majesty's Army. It was before I became your aide. There was some unrest in the Balkans, and I was posted with an observation unit there. My job was to deliver reports on the situation to London. I had to pass through many villages as I went back and forth several times. One night, I passed through a village along a mountain pass in Germany. I believe it was called Hochheim. In one area outside of the village, I saw a blue fog like this."

"Certainly this is just some strange weather condition," observed Morrison. "I wonder what's causing it?"

"Watch how it moves, and there is no wind to push it along," Johnstone commented. "It's compact in the middle and stretched out on the left and right sides."

"Yes, I see it. Look, it's drifting towards shore," observed Morrison.

"I don't know if it's drifting, Sir," Potter conjectured.

"What do you mean?" asked Morrison.

"See the two parts of the fog that are stretched out? See them waving gently up and down? It appears as if it's slowly flying to the shore!"

"What?" Johnstone said in disbelief. "It probably just appears that way from the angle in which we are observing this."

"Well," Morrison said, "whatever it's doing, it looks like it's heading towards Whitechapel!"

"Let's get back to High Street," suggested Johnstone.

The three men quickly returned to the central area of the district. The number of people in the area had not diminished since they left. More trash had accumulated, however, and a few more drunkards had passed out from their overindulgence. Down the street, they could see the blue fog approaching.

"This is very odd," Johnstone observed.

No one else seemed to be taking notice of the phenomenon. The three men walked towards the encroaching fog, and soon found themselves surrounded by it. As it made contact with the men, the fog seemed to pause for just a moment before it left them and continued drifting down the street.

"Did you smell that?" asked Morrison after the fog had passed.

"Yes, I did," Johnstone confirmed.

"Yes, I did too," added Potter. "It smelled like lilac!"

"Where did it go?" asked Morrison.

"I think it drifted into an alley a few blocks away from here," Potter said.

"Let's go see if we can track it further," Morrison suggested.

They started in the direction they had seen the fog move. They advanced at a quick pace, often pushing their way through the people standing about. They walked into the dark, dead-end alley.

"Damn!" exclaimed Morrison. "We're too late. It's not here!"

"Where could it have gone?" asked Potter.

"I don't know," Johnstone replied. "Fog just doesn't disappear like that."

"Well, interesting as it's been," said Morrison, "I don't think there's much else we can do here tonight. Is there anything else either of you think we should do?"

"No, I think you're right. Our purpose in coming to Whitechapel tonight was to get an idea of what activities go on here. I think I have a better understanding of the situation now," Johnstone stated and shook his head.

"All right then. Let's return to my carriage and I'll take you home. We can get back together in a couple of days for tea, say Tuesday, and discuss our next actions?"

"That sounds good to me," Johnstone said.

They turned to leave the alley.

"Shh," Potter stopped them. "Listen!" he whispered.

From the back of the alley, they heard footsteps coming towards them. Turning, they saw a figure approaching.

"I didn't see anything back there when we arrived here, did you?" asked Morrison softly.

"Not me, but it is dark in the back and hard to see anything," Johnstone said.

The figure continued to approach. It was a man, not quite

middle-aged. He was clean, with a strong build, and well dressed in a cloak and top hat. He face was tilted down.

"Good evening, gentlemen," he said, and tipped his hat slightly to them as he passed. He carefully avoided eye contact and walked from the alley onto the street.

"That was odd," said Morrison. "Where did he come from? And his accent…Eastern European, I think."

"Yes. Sounded Romanian to me," Johnstone pondered. "He could have been hiding in a doorway or alcove back there." He then sniffed the air. "Do you smell lilac?"

"Yes I do!" Morrison answered.

"If he was hiding," Potter said, "do you think…"

"Quickly!" exclaimed Morrison.

"What is it?" Johnstone asked.

"Potter, you go to the street and keep an eye on our friend. William, we need to check every corner of this alley!"

Potter ran to the street to keep the man in view. The other two men stumbled about in the dark alley. Each took a different side. When necessary, they would light a match to illuminate an area of the alley before moving on. The alley was relatively short and they quickly completed their task.

"Thank God!" said a much-relieved Johnstone.

"Yes," agreed Morrison. "I thought for sure we'd find a body or something in here. Let's go find Potter."

They walked back to the street and found Potter not far from the alley. He was standing close to a building in an attempt to conceal himself.

"Where's our friend?" Morrison asked.

"Did you find anything?" Potter asked in return.

"No, everything seemed to be all right back there."

"That's good." Potter said in a relieved tone. "I've been watching him. He's just walking down the street."

"What is he doing?" asked Morrison.

"Not much. Sometimes he looks about at the people, but he doesn't …Wait a second…"

"What is it?" Morrison asked.

"He just stopped and is talking to a woman outside of a pub… Looks like she works at that location. I saw her standing there when we came over to the alley."

"Do you think we can move towards him without his detecting us?" Morrison was getting anxious.

"I believe so if we stay close to the buildings…Wait! He's walking off with her!"

"Which way are they going?" Morrison asked, his anxiety level increasing as Potter continued to report.

"They're walking down the sidewalk away from where we are."

"All right then," Morrison said. "Potter, you keep vigilance and start towards him. Don't get too close or you'll give yourself away! We'll be walking a few paces behind you. If you think he's about to do anything, start after him. When we see you move after him, we'll quicken our pace as well."

They began their cautious pursuit of the suspect, who was casually walking arm-in-arm with the woman he met. The couple continued walking for a few more blocks and then turned into another dead end alley. When they turned, Potter began to run towards their location. The other two men saw Potter's action and quickly followed him. When Potter approached the alley, he slowed and walked to the corner of the pub that stood at the intersection. Morrison and Johnstone met Potter there.

"What do you see?" Johnstone asked breathlessly, as Potter peeked down the alley.

Potter turned back towards the men and answered, "It's extremely dark and hard to see. There are very few gas lamps in this district. However, it looks like the woman is leaning against a building and he's kissing her."

"Kissing her?" Morrison repeated.

"Yes," Potter confirmed, "he started on the lips, and is now kissing her neck."

"Doesn't sound like a murderer to me," Johnstone commented. "Besides, there was a murder just last night. Seems too soon…"

"No!" exclaimed Potter, interrupting Johnstone.

"What is it?" Morrison hastily inquired.

"She's collapsed to the ground!"

"Are you sure?"

"Yes! What are we going to do?"

"William, go find a constable, police officer or any other official who can help. Potter, you and I will go and see what happened, and see if we can do anything for that woman!"

They were about to perform as Morrison instructed, but stopped suddenly as they were startled by the emergence of their suspect from the alley.

"Good evening, gentlemen," he spoke to them in the same manner as before, with his voice sounding almost as if in recognition of the three. Once again, he was careful to avoid eye contact with the men.

Forgetting Morrison's previous instructions, all three ran to the woman as their suspect walked out of the alley. She was sitting on the sidewalk. Her clothing, though somewhat soiled, was orderly and not torn. She seemed partially dazed, but grew more alert as she heard the three men rushing up to her. Seeing their silhouettes against the light from High Street, she became alarmed and began to scream. The echoes of her terror resounded off the buildings in the alley.

A whistle answered her scream and soon the three men and the woman found themselves surrounded by four police officers. The bull's eye lanterns were pointed at the faces of the men.

One of the officers broke the silence as he instructed another to check on the condition of the woman. Then he turned his attention to the men. "All right, gentlemen…What's all this then?"

V.

"Well, all I can say now," Johnstone lamented as they rode back to his cottage in Morrison's carriage, "is that we certainly botched things tonight! At least you had your letter from Sir Charles with you. We'd most likely all be in bloody jail right now if you hadn't. I will definitely carry my letter from now on!"

"A very embarrassing moment indeed," Potter commented.

"What's worse," a dejected Morrison responded, "is that we never got any information about our suspect, and we never had a chance to talk to the young woman."

"He has also seen us twice now," Johnstone observed. "That will make it difficult for us to follow him in the future, if we ever chance upon him again."

"So," Potter asked, "what happens next?"

"We should probably not return to Whitechapel until after we talk to Sir Charles," Johnstone suggested.

"Oh, bloody hell!" Morrison exclaimed. "You can believe that first thing in the morning Sir Charles will get a full report on our activities from tonight!" Morrison thought a moment, and then concluded, "William, we won't have to worry about when to talk to Sir Charles about this. I'm certain he'll invite us all very soon to his office for a talk."

"Do you think he'll ask us to step down?" Potter asked.

"More demand than ask, I'd wager," Morrison replied.

"Look over at the river," Johnstone interrupted as they made a turn in the road. "This fog travels all over."

"One of the strangest things I've ever seen," Morrison remarked, as they looked upon the blue fog hovering over the water. "What is it?"

"Hmm," Potter sounded. "We may have to think differently about this."

"How so?" Morrison asked.

"It may not be so much what it IS, but rather what's IN it?"

***

Just as Colonel Morrison predicted, on the following Monday morning all three men received a letter from Sir Charles that was delivered by police courier. They were directed to appear in his office at noon on Wednesday, the fifth day of September.

Johnstone and Potter arrived together while Morrison came in his own carriage. They were escorted to Sir Charles' office, and were instructed to sit in the meeting chairs in front of the desk until Sir Charles arrived. The three men, looking as if they were young schoolboys sent to the master's office, waited as told. A slight nervousness was contained within them that manifested itself through some uncontrolled fidgeting as they tried to sit still. They did not talk to each other, and their gazes were focused on the floor like criminals awaiting sentencing from a judge.

The office was large considering Sir Charles' position with the Metropolitan Police. The furniture was finely made from good wood. There were several shelves filled with various legal books and other material. His desk contained stacks of paper and folders.

What paperwork was not in view was kept secured in filing cabinets that lined the back wall. A picture of Queen Victoria hung on the wall and the Union Jack was positioned in the right corner of the room behind his desk.

In a delay that was probably pre-calculated, Sir Charles arrived in his office fifteen minutes later. The men started to rise from their chairs when he entered his office, but he motioned to them to remain seated. He sat down in the chair behind his desk, picked up and then read what the three presumed was the report on their activities from the previous night. They remained silent throughout the wait.

Sir Charles shook his head; his cheeks were slightly flushed. He looked up at them and began, "Gentlemen, perhaps I wasn't very clear with you during our meeting last week." He looked at all three one by one, and then in a stern tone continued, "So let me make certain that we fully understand what it is that I am asking you to do for me." He repeated their instructions. "You are to listen to the talk on the street, in the public houses, taverns and any other places where people are gathered. I need all the information that is possible to obtain regarding these murders. When you learn something new that may help the investigation, you are to provide it to me as soon as possible. You will report all suspicious activity that you observe directly to any law enforcement personnel in the area at the time. That is the extent of your charge, gentlemen. Let me finish by saying that in no uncertain terms are you to make an apprehension on your own initiative. If you encounter the suspect, call for the constable and see to any victim's well being, if there is one."

When he finished, Sir Charles ask the three if they understood their charge. Johnstone and Potter quickly acknowledged their understanding of what they had been told. Morrison, on the other hand, wanted to participate in as active a role as the police. He did not voice that opinion to Sir Charles, however, and delayed his response. He looked over at Johnstone and Potter, and gave them a slight grin. He then turned back to Sir Charles and indicated his acceptance of the instructions.

Sir Charles had a busy schedule for the remainder of the day, and had no time for further discussion. He dismissed them and resumed his normal duties.

VI.

Johnstone, Morrison and Potter left Scotland Yard and went to Colonel Morrison's home. Believing that they were on a sort of parole, they discussed plans for returning to the East End to continue their surveillance activities. When nightfall was complete, they returned to Whitechapel.

Johnstone, Morrison and Potter were dressed in less formal attire than they had been on the first night that they ventured into the district. They found that this permitted them to mingle more with the people in the area. However, they heard little talk about the three murders. This was something that frustrated Morrison. He mentioned to his two companions that perhaps they needed to dress even more like those who lived in the district to get the people to accept them as residents and speak freely.

As it neared midnight, the three men were tiring and becoming disappointed over their inability to obtain any information. They decided to leave, and were walking back towards Morrison's carriage when they saw the blue fog floating above High Street. It floated towards them in the same manner as it had the previous night.

"What the hell kind of a fog is this?" Johnstone asked.

"I don't know," said an energized Morrison, "but when we last saw a fog like that, things got exciting!"

"And we got into trouble," reminded Potter.

"It'll be all right this time," Morrison assured.

As the fog came nearer, it moved upwards and floated above

them as it passed, but it did not come in contact them. They watched as it drifted into the same alley as it had the first night that they were in Whitechapel.

"Coincidence?" Morrison asked.

"I doubt that," Johnstone replied. "I don't know of any weather system that reacts like that just did. It seemed to intentionally elevate itself to avoid contacting us."

"Then let's go see what's going on in that alley tonight," suggested Morrison.

Before they could start towards the alley, however, they saw the same well-dressed man in topcoat and hat emerge from it.

"Now, there's our friend from the other night," Morrison observed. "There's a connection between him and what's going on around here. I'm sure of it."

"But what is his involvement?" Potter asked.

"Yes," interjected Johnstone, "he's too well groomed for this locale, even if he's wearing the same clothes from the last time we saw him."

"Then let's watch him and find out what his intentions are," Morrison stated. "That's what our task is, isn't it?"

They watched as their suspect repeated his actions from the other night. This included approaching the very same woman whom he had met on the night that they first encountered him. The two talked for a moment and then walked away together in the direction of the same alley that he had previously taken her.

"I'll go find a policeman," Potter stated.

"What for?" Morrison asked.

"To report this suspicious man like we were told to do."

Morrison shook his head. "Potter, you're going to tell a policeman that you saw a man hire a prostitute in Whitechapel? A police report in a recent *Times* stated that there are almost two thousand prostitutes and almost one hundred brothels in Whitechapel alone. I doubt you'll get anyone to consider that as something suspicious here."

"But we were told…"

"Don't worry about Sir Charles," Morrison interrupted. "He said what he was required to say. We'll be all right. Trust me. When the time is right, we'll contact the police."

"I have to agree with Colonel Morrison," Johnstone stated. "Going to the police now won't do any good." He turned to Morrison, and asked, "All right then, Thomas, what do you suggest we do now?"

Morrison contemplated for a few seconds, and then offered his suggestion. "We're on the other side of the street from him this time. We'll follow him from this side. If he goes into another alley like the other night, maybe we can see what he's doing from where we are."

"Sounds safe to me," Johnstone said.

They followed their suspect. Consistent with his movements of the previous encounter, he and his female companion entered the alley together.

"All right, Potter," Morrison instructed, "you cross the street and see if you can spot a policeman. Don't let our friend see you! If we see something happening other than what we'd expect from this sort of transaction, we'll wave our arms. If you see us do that, you get the policeman, and we'll run across the street and into the alley to stop whatever he's doing."

"Very well, Sir." Potter acknowledged, as he left and crossed the street while the other two remained behind and watched the couple in the dark alley.

"Can you make out what they're doing, William?"

"No, it's too dark in the back of the alley where they are."

"Then we had better cross and get a better view."

"All right, but we need to be careful."

The two began crossing the street.

"I can see a little bit better into the alley," Johnstone said. "Looks to me like they're kissing." He continued to watch, as they were midway across the street. "Yes, that's what they're doing. Just kissing…Now he's kissing her on the neck." Johnstone suddenly became alarmed. "Wait! Something just happened!" he exclaimed. "She's fallen to the ground!"

"Come on! Let's get over there!"cried Morrison.

They waved at Potter as they made their way across the rest of the street. Potter held up his arms as if to say that he was unable to find a police officer, and moved quickly toward the alley to join Johnstone and Morrison. They ran into the alley. Not seeing their suspect, they slowed their approach. They hoped that by not storming onto the scene they would not set the woman into a panic as they had the first time they saw her.

"Where did he go?" asked Morrison.

"I don't know," answered Potter.

"We were right here," said Johnstone. "Did either of you see him come out of the alley? Damn it, he would have had to pass right by us!"

"I didn't see anyone come out," Potter replied.

"He may be hiding," Morrison conjectured, "so be careful. I'll check the woman and see if she's all right. You two check the rest of the alley. At least it has a dead end."

As Johnstone and Potter began their search of the area, Morrison slowly approached the woman. She appeared to be more dazed and less coherent than she had been the first night they saw her.

"Wha...no..." she shook her head and started to speak when she noticed Morrison approaching. "You...no!" she weakly spoke and tried to move away from him.

"Shh," whispered Morrison as he knelt down in front of her.

"Leave me alone!" she pleaded in an agitated manner, but her voice was still not loud enough to alert anyone outside of the alley.

"It's all right, my dear," Morrison tried to calm her. "My friends and I are here to help you. Are you all right?"

Johnstone and Potter came running up to Morrison and the woman. She cowered and unsuccessfully tried to push herself away.

"It's all right," Morrison tried to assure her. "They're friends of mine. They were trying to find the man who was just here with you."

"Man?" she asked. "Man with me? Here? What man?"

"Yes, the man you were with in this alley."

"I not a man remember," she replied, then paused and looked up at Morrison. "Why I feel afraid?"

Morrison turned to Johnstone, and asked, "Did you find anything?"

"Nothing. I don't understand it. I heard a noise and thought there was someone hiding in a doorway at the back of the alley. Turned out to be just a bat fluttering about."

"Is she all right?" asked Potter.

"She seems to be a bit dazed and confused about what's going on here," Morrison answered. "I don't know if she understands me."

"Why not?" Johnstone asked.

"From her accent, I think she's Russian. I'm not sure if she understands much English."

"Let me try," Johnstone offered as he knelt down in front of the woman. "Molodaya ledi," Johnstone began.

"Thomas, I didn't know you could speak Russian!" Morrison exclaimed.

"Learned it in India," he replied and then turned his attention back to the woman. "What's your name?" he continued in Russian.

She looked up at Johnstone and tried to find the answer. "Name?" was all that she could say, but her response was in English.

"Yes," Morrison joined in. "What's your name?"

"My name…" The simple question began to bring her mind back in focus. "My name…Vio…Violetta…" Her voice came back along with her memory. "That man…"

"Do you remember him?" Morrison eagerly asked.

"Give her a moment, Thomas," Johnstone tried to calm Morrison's exuberance. "I believe she's coming around."

"That man," she repeated.

"Yes," Morrison said, "who was that man?"

"I was on my pitch…" She rubbed her head with her hand and then continued, "What I doing here?"

"That's what we're trying to figure out as well, Miss," Johnstone said. "Do you feel strong enough to stand up and walk out to the street?"

She nodded and tried, but could not regain her footing.

"Here," Johnstone offered. "Grab my hand and I'll help you up."

As she stood, she was somewhat unsteady. Morrison helped by getting hold of her other arm. They held her as she regained her balance.

"Oh, my head hurts," Violetta said, as she put her hand on her forehead. She noticed that the three men were looking intently at her. "Now you men go away and leave me alone! I not pissed! I did not have any drink. I just work my pitch!"

"That's all right," Johnstone said calmly. "We just want to help you. Do you think you can walk back to the street?"

"Yes, I think with little help. Then I be right. Thank you."

They walked slowly out of the alley with Johnstone and Morrison holding her up. Potter followed closely behind. At the corner, she stopped at a lamppost, let go of their hands and held on to it for support.

"I so tired," she sighed.

Underneath the lit gas lamp, the men were able to get their first good look at her. She appeared to be relatively clean and well groomed. She had a pleasing figure, a youthful, but very pale face and long flowing auburn hair.

"Would you like to go sit down inside the pub to rest a bit?" Johnstone asked.

"It not my pitch," she answered a little stronger. "The girls there not like my being on their pitch. They not like Russian."

"Well," spoke Morrison, "considering your condition and what just happened to you, I think anyone can make allowances and show some latitude towards you tonight. Besides," Morrison smiled at her, "I think I could use a little nip after all this!"

Violetta smiled slightly at his remark, but started to lose her grip on the pole. Morrison and Johnstone caught her before she could fall.

"I guess I need go and sit down as you say. I not think I make it to my pitch right now."

"Let's get her out of the street," Potter said, as he observed people beginning to take notice of the four. "I'll make some room to make it easier for us to get through the crowd."

A little pushing and shoving ensued, but no one prevented their entering the pub. It was noisy, old, dirty and filled with people in various states of dress and drunkenness. The wooden plank floor emitted a faint urine odor. They found a small table near the front door and convinced the people already there to vacate it for them.

A barmaid came up to their table as they seated themselves. "The girls are not going to take this well with you in here, Missy!" she warned.

Morrison interjected, "This woman is sick. We brought her in here so she could rest a moment before we move along."

"Whatever you say, Governor, but they aren't going to be happy with your lot in here." She looked at Violetta, and continued, "Here now, what the bloody hell did you gents do to her anyway?"

"Madame," Johnstone was incensed, "how dare you insinuate that we would harm this woman! We did nothing of the kind. We're trying to help her!" he concluded defiantly.

"All right! All right! What's all this?" came the high-pitched voice of another woman as she pushed her way towards the table.

Two other women were accompanying her.

"I told you they wouldn't take kindly to this," the barmaid confirmed. "I'll fetch the proprietor presently. There'll be no fightin' in here!"

"Get out of my way, you damn blokes!" the woman yelled at a couple of sailors. "Let me get at that table!"

"I told you bringing her in here would come to no good. There'll be no fightin' in here!" the barmaid repeated as she left to bring the owner.

"Get out of my way, you wench!" the woman, obviously drunk, yelled as she pushed her way past the barmaid.

"Annie, there'll be no fightin'!" the barmaid instructed as she went the find the owner.

Swaying from drink, with the other two women standing

behind her, she stood over the table as best she could. Annie was in her forties. She was short and stout, with blue eyes and short, dark wavy hair. She was dressed in dark, soiled clothing. Her companions were also intoxicated. One was in her thirties and was tall and slim with long, wavy hair. The other was a stark contrast to the others as she was clean, well dressed, younger and very attractive.

"All right, Dearie," Annie started, "you know the rules 'bout bringing gents into our pitch!"

"Look, Miss…" Morrison started, but was interrupted.

"I'm not talking to you blokes! I'm talking to your damn Russian whore!" Annie yelled in a drunken, slurred tone.

"Get this sot out of here!" Johnstone demanded.

Morrison stood and unintentionally bumped into the woman. The action caused her to stagger away from the table and almost fall to the floor.

"Here, you watch yourself, Mister!" one of her companions warned.

Annie balanced herself. "Lizzie, I can handle this bloke! You stay back. You too, Mary Jane!"

"We don't take kindly to men pushing us about the place!" Lizzie, who spoke with a Swedish accent, interjected.

Morrison grabbed hold of Annie's arm and escorted her near the door to the pub.

"Here, what you think you're doing to her?" Mary Jane called out to him, speaking with a slight Irish accent.

"I will return her to you directly," Morrison instructed. "You two just stay there for now."

Near the door, he spoke sternly to Annie in a volume that was just below that of the ambient noise level in the pub, "Now, Annie, you listen to me and you listen very carefully. That girl we are with needs to rest here for a little while. We're staying until she regains her strength and can leave on her own."

"But this is not her pitch, and she has no right in here with her gents!"

"We're not her 'gents'. We're only trying to help her."

"Well, she's not staying, no matter!"

"All right," Morrison reached into his pocket, took out a coin and gave it to Annie. "Will this satisfy you for our trespass here tonight?"

"Half a crown!" she exclaimed, and then thought. "And my friends?"

He reached in his pocket and produced two more coins.

"Governor, you can stay all here night! I'll even give you a turn, too, if you want! I'm sure the other ladies will take care of your friends too, if they want. We're much better than any Russian girl, if you know what I mean."

"That will be quite all right, Miss. I will have to respectfully decline your offer, and I'm sure my friends will do likewise. We are not interested in taking a 'turn' with you or your friends. We only want to help the young lady."

"Whatever you say, Governor. One night you'll want us, and we'll be here, or in another pub just down the street," she winked.

At that moment, the proprietor walked up, "Is there a problem here, Annie?"

"No problem, Jack. No problem at all!" She turned back to Morrison, and held up the coin, "Thank you, Love." She tried to hug and kiss Morrison, but he avoided her advance. She shrugged at the rejection. "If you or your friends change your minds and want a go, we'll be in the back." She turned and staggered away towards the bar.

As she rejoined the other women, she motioned for them to follow her. She gave one of the coins to each. When seeing the coin, Mary Jane began singing an Irish ballad. They went over to the bar, where Annie yelled at the bartender to give her another drink. They then returned to their table.

Jack looked at Morrison, "I don't want any more problems here tonight, if you know what I mean. Don't ever bring your Russian friend in here again, or I'll bounce every one of you out of here myself. Do we understand each other?"

"Quite," Morrison answered indignantly, as he turned and walked back to the table to rejoin the others.

In the meantime, Violetta had regained her composure.

"Well, you certainly look much better than when we brought you in here," Morrison observed as he sat back down.

"Yes, thank you. Your friends tell me what happen. I remember not much of it."

"William," Johnstone started, "I took the liberty of ordering a round of ales for us, and some food for our hungry young lady."

"Well, I certainly need this tonight!" Morrison gratefully said as he took a pull from the mug.

"Thomas," Johnstone began, "you were right, she is from Russia. Moscow to be exact. So, let me introduce you to Miss Violetta Karanova."

Morrison stood, took her right hand and kissed it, "A pleasure to meet you Miss Karanova," he pronounced and reseated himself.

"Is everything settled with those ladies?" asked Johnstone as he motioned with his head to the back of the pub.

"Nothing I couldn't handle, William," Morrison responded, as he took another drink from the mug. He turned to Violetta, "Do you want anything to drink to wash down that stew, my dear?"

"No," she replied, "I try never drink too much. I get crazy when I drink."

Morrison shook his head, "You certainly are not what I had expected…"

"Of woman like me?" she interrupted.

"Well, uh," Morrison stammered, "forgive me, Miss Karanova, it's just that I thought..."

"I be like Annie and others here?"

"Well, to put it frankly, yes, that's right."

"Annie likes the drink. I was married to English sailor who liked the drink too. I had child, and he became mean with the drink. He ran off with other woman."

"Well, uh, so it's actually Mrs. then, right?" Morrison asked.

"Miss is right," she replied, obviously flattered by the formality of the men towards her. "My husband, he was killed in fight many months back. When he die, I take back my name."

"Please, Miss Karanova, accept my apology for presuming you

to be what you obviously are not."

"No need apologize," she commented. "Most men come here looking for fancy, and they not care what or who she be. I do what I do for my little girl. There no work here in district for Russian woman. Too many people here. We have to eat or starve."

The table grew quiet as the men took several pulls from their drinks to dispel the awkwardness of the moment.

Morrison cleared his throat, breaking the silence, and then asked, "Miss Karanova, do you remember anything that happened to you tonight?"

She shook her head, "I remember seeing gentleman walk towards me at my pitch. He look familiar to me, but I not sure that I see him before tonight."

"Do you remember seeing him last week?"

"No, and I not remember anything after he walk up to me."

"This is very strange," mused Morrison.

"And Thomas, look at this," Johnstone said.

Violetta's dress had a high lace collar.

"Miss Karanova, if you'd permit me," Johnstone said, as he turned down the left side of the collar.

"What the devil is that?" Morrison asked, as he leaned towards her to get a closer view. "It looks like two puncture wounds on her neck!"

"Exactly," Johnstone replied. "They appear to be fresh, but not newly inflicted tonight."

"What are you saying?" Morrison asked. "Where's the blood? Her collar should have blood stains."

"It's the mark of a vampire," Potter said.

"What?" exclaimed Johnstone.

"Are you daft, Potter? Vampires?"Morrison rebutted the comment. "Those are just old legends."

"I beg to differ with you, Sir," Potter argued.

"Ridiculous, Potter!" Morrison chided. "I supposed next you'll say that there's a werewolf loose in London!"

"You can make fun of me over this, but I tell you, Sir, this is the sign of a vampire, and the gentleman that we've been watching…"

"Is a vampire?" Johnstone interrupted.

"Yes."

Morrison shook his head and asked, "What makes you so sure?"

Violetta was listening intently to the discussion.

"I told you that years ago I was in Germany and saw a blue fog. In Hochheim, the village I passed through, many of the people spoke of such things. They were tormented by a vampire one winter not so long ago."

"All right," Morrison conjectured, "if you are correct, and if we are following a vampire, is this the same one from Germany, and is this the murderer we're looking for?"

"I don't know," Potter answered. "They are powerful beings, though, and not much is beyond their capabilities."

"My God!" Violetta exclaimed. "You say man who took me to alley was vampire?"

"Yes," responded Potter. "I don't have any doubt of that, and I believe that he also has taken you many times before and is feeding on you now."

"For what purpose he do this?"

"To live, Miss Karanova. Vampires feed on the blood of the living so that they can keep their dead hearts alive. Then, when their victim becomes too weak to sustain them, the vampire takes their life force, and the victim becomes a vampire condemned for eternity with their sire."

"Oh come now, Potter," interjected Morrison. "You are going to scare Miss Karanova."

"No, I not scared. In Russia, many stories of vampire in Europe. Mister Potter, you say he feed off me, and is going to kill me?" She was becoming agitated despite what she told Morrison. "And you think he kill other girls, and they now vampires?"

"All of what you said is possible," Potter said. "But, we don't have enough evidence or information right now to answer your questions. I'm sorry."

Violetta stood; the men rose with her.

She smiled in acknowledgement of their manners, looked at them, and said, "I not think I want hear any more of this! Why he feed on me? I nothing to him. I just try take care of my girl."

"Please sit, Miss Karanova," Morrison requested.

"You nice men. You help me. No one ever help before. I much better now, and think I can go. I need go back to my pitch and work. Probably someone already there. I have to fight her off it."

"Please," Morrison requested again, "I implore you to stay. We need to talk to you more about what happened."

"You nice men helping girl like me," she repeated. "No one do that here. No one care here. But I now must go."

She walked off and left the pub. The three were disappointed over losing their first good lead in their investigation. Johnstone and Morrison blamed Potter for scaring her off with his talk of vampires.

Not expecting any further activity for the night, they decided to leave the district. They rose and heard a whistle emanating from the back of the pub. As they looked, Annie held up her mug and waved. Lizzie was in the arms of a sailor, and Mary Jane was loudly singing her Irish ballad.

They rode back to Morrison's home where Johnstone and Potter retrieved their carriage and rode back to the cottage. As they had observed previously on the road to their home, the blue fog was present, hovering over the river.

"Potter, what do you think is the purpose of this fog? Seeing and watching it as it swirls and moves about is like a dream. It's hypnotizing. Yet, I get the impression that there's something more to it. Our friend is involved, and what is his connection with Miss Karanova?"

Potter shrugged his shoulders, "We just don't have enough information yet."

"We'd better find out more soon, before someone else dies. I would hate to find out that Miss Karanova was the next victim."

The next morning, Morrison went to Scotland Yard to report what they had observed in the district. However, he made no mention of vampires to Sir Charles.

VII.

The energized volunteer investigators returned to the Whitechapel District on Friday night, the seventh day of September. They had decided to conduct their investigation this night at a later hour so that they could observe the people who were active in the area after midnight. They arrived in the central part of the district, where they had been on their previous visits. Johnstone commented on the weather and the noticeable lack of any fog.

"Good!" chimed Morrison, "One less thing to distract us!"

They went first to the area where they believed Violetta would be. They spotted her at what they had learned was her normal location to conduct business, but they were on the opposite side of the street. They remained at their position and watched her. Many men passed by without giving her much of a glance. At times, she appeared to be pleading with them and sometimes even grabbed a man's arm to try to hold him for a moment while trying to plead her situation, only to be easily pushed aside.

Even from their location, they could see that Violetta was noticeably weaker than when they last saw her just two nights ago. Her face and hands, the only parts of her body that were exposed to the chilly September night, were extremely pale, appearing almost translucent. Her clothing and hair were disheveled, in sharp contrast to her mostly orderly appearance on the night that they talked in the pub.

"There he is!" Potter pointed as the man they had seen with

Violetta walked out of the alley and continued towards her.

"He didn't need any fog tonight, Potter," Morrison chided.

"Maybe he was already in the alley before we arrived and was waiting for the right moment to appear," Potter countered.

"Why would he need to wait for anything? Miss Karanova is standing on the corner, and probably has been there all night. He could go there any time he wanted. No one around here takes much notice of anything from what I have seen."

"He certainly is brazen in his constant approach to that poor woman," said Johnstone.

Potter added, "I'll wager he's been seeing her every night like this for at least a week. That's probably why she looks so emaciated."

They watched as the scene repeated itself almost exactly as they had witnessed twice before. They resolved to confront their suspect in the alley before he could do any further harm to Violetta. Potter advised the others that they should advance with extreme caution.

As the man approached Violetta, she reached out to him as she had other passersby, but her entreaties quickly stopped. She stood still; her gaze was fixated on him as she was in a trance. The man put her hand on his right arm and they walked away together towards the alley adjacent to the pub. The three observers set a quick pace as they followed.

They crossed the street as the couple turned into the alley. Just as the men reached the corner, a fight erupted from within the pub and boiled out onto the sidewalk and street. Bystanders not involved in the altercation took advantage of the opportunity to join in the fracas, turning the entire scene into one large, drunken brawl.

"Damn!" exclaimed Morrison. "This rabble is blocking our way! We've got to get through and get to the alley quickly!"

Pushing and shoving their way through the riotous crowd, they sustained several hits to different parts of their bodies, but made it through in relatively short order, and as the police whistles began blowing from many directions.

They turned the corner and entered the alley. The man was holding Violetta, as if her body was too weak to stand on its own. His head was turned at an angle, and it appeared as if he was kissing her neck.

"You there!" Potter called out challenging him. "Stop!"

The man looked up at them and released his grip on Violetta. She collapsed onto the dirt-covered sidewalk. He turned to face them as they advanced closer, emitting a low growl as he peered at the three. His piercing eyes glowed a bright red as he advanced to confront them.

"We need to take him and see to the girl!" Johnstone said, as the three stopped.

"No!" objected Potter, as the man neared their position. "He's much too strong for us to do that. We'll never take him!"

"We must do some..." Morrison's voice drifted off as he fell under the man's hypnotic gaze.

"What's happening to Morrison?" asked Johnstone.

"Stand back, Sir!" Potter ordered. "Do not look at his eyes, no matter what you see!"

Potter stepped forward, placing himself between the other two and their adversary.

"You will not succeed here, my friend," Potter said, as he turned his attention to the man.

"I already have," he growled, as he continued his approach. He was now just a few yards away. He had Morrison in a controlling trance and then turned his hypnotic gaze to Potter.

Potter felt the power from within the man's eyes begin to burn inside of him. He quickly diverted his eyes towards the ground. He put his hand into his jacket pocket and produced a bright, metal crucifix.

"No, you will not succeed!" Potter decreed, as he held up the religious icon at eye level with the man.

The adversary stopped his approach, gave a quick shriek in unexpected alarm and turned his eyes away.

"You know not in what you are involving yourselves!" he warned in a deep voice. "Stay out of this!"

With the hypnotic gaze on Morrison now broken for too long, the hapless victim fell to the cobblestones. He was still dazed from the trance as Johnstone hurried to him. Potter maintained his position and held up the crucifix in full view of the menacing beast.

The man growled in contempt and continued, "This night you have had the better play, but be forewarned. I shall continue to taste British blood until my task is complete. Stay out from underfoot and maybe I won't taste yours!"

With those words, he transformed himself into a bat and flew away.

Johnstone had been tending to Morrison, but saw the transformation. With the being's departure, he instructed Potter to check on Violetta's condition. Potter ran the short distance into the alley where Violetta lay.

"How is she?" Johnstone called out.

Violetta lay unconscious. Potter found her to be extremely pale. Her breathing was very shallow and her pulse was faint.

"Colonel, we need to get her to hospital as soon as possible or I fear she will not survive!" Potter called back to Johnstone.

"Understood," Johnstone responded. "Thomas, are you all right?"

"I…I think so, William."

"All right then. You wait here. I have to find a carriage to take Miss Karanova and you to hospital!"

Johnstone ran out of the alley and stood at the now quiet street corner. The fight had long been quelled. He surmised that the lack of any police presence was due to their having taken away many of those involved in the fight. He spotted someone moving an empty lorry down High Street. He hailed the driver, told him of the need and quickly hired it. The driver brought the lorry into the alley and helped place Morrison and Violetta into it. Johnstone climbed onboard and instructed Potter to retrieve Morrison's carriage, and meet them at the hospital.

By the time they arrived at the hospital Morrison had regained most of his composure, but had only a vague memory of what had transpired in the alley. Violetta remained unconscious, and was taken immediately to a room for treatment. Another doctor examined Morrison, but found nothing wrong with him.

Potter arrived shortly thereafter. They tried to see Violetta, but were not permitted to do so. The doctor informed them, however, that she was not expected to survive to the morning.

All three were exhausted from the ordeal. Morrison convinced Johnstone and Potter to take his carriage, return to his home and inform his wife what had happened. Then they should return to their home to rest. He would stay at the hospital to monitor Violetta's condition. Later in the morning, they should return to the hospital to take him home. There was nothing that they could do in the interim. Morrison said that he would update them as soon as they returned.

***

At four in the morning on the eighth day of September, three intoxicated women exited the Queen's Head Pub, and stood on the corner underneath the lamppost. One was singing an Irish ballad, while another had her arms around a man whom she had met in the pub.

"Mary Jane, do you have to sing that song all the time, and so loudly too?" asked the third woman.

"Annie, I sing it when I'm happy," Mary Jane replied.

"But don't you know any other song that you can sing?"

"It's a nice song, and I sing it when I'm happy. Right now, I am happy!"

"Bother that!" Annie retorted.

"Oh, Annie, leave the girl alone," Lizzie responded. Her drunken male companion tugged on her. "Easy, Love. You'll have your fun soon enough."

Annie laughed, "Lizzie, you'd better move along!"

"Yes," slurred the male, "I'm ready, Lizzie. Let's have a turn!"

"Oh, all right, Love, let's get on with it then. Come on. There's a spot not far up the road where we can go."

Lizzie and her companion departed. Annie and Mary Jane made their farewells to each other, and left in separate directions towards their homes. Mary Jane resumed singing her song, to which Annie only shook her head. Only a few seconds departed from each other, Annie heard Mary Jane's singing cease. She stopped and turned. She could hear Mary Jane speaking with a man.

"Good evening Mr. Hutchinson!" Mary Jane greeted.

"More like the morning, Miss Kelly," he returned.

George Hutchinson was about thirty years old, and was short and stout. He lived at a men's home on Commercial Street. Hutchinson and Kelly were familiar to each other. Although he never purchased her favors, he was often seen with her.

"Oh, forgive me. I didn't realize it was so late."

"Quite all right, Miss Kelly."

"Are you on your way home, Mr. Hutchinson?"

"Yes, as a matter of fact, I am."

"Then would you mind walking with me to mine?"

"Not at all, Miss Kelly. Anything for a pretty lass."

She put her hand on his arm and they began walking to her home. Annie knew that that the two lived close to each other, and Hutchinson would make sure that Mary Jane arrived home safely.

Annie turned and continued homeward. A couple of blocks in the distance, she saw a blue fog appear upon the street. It moved away and turned into an alley located on the same side of the street where she was walking. As she reached that location, she stopped and looked into it. The alley was dark and not well lit. She could see nothing. Then she heard some movement.

"Who's there?" she called.

"Just me, Miss. Do you need something?" A constable walked out of the alley.

"Oh no, Sir. I just saw something come into the alley, and then heard you. Just trying to be safe."

"Very well, Miss. oing home now, are you?"

"Yes, Sir."

"All right, then. Mind your way."

"Thank you, Sir."

The constable stood at the corner as Annie resumed walking. Another block down the road she saw a figure standing in a dark, recessed doorway.

"How are you this day?"

Annie stopped at the greeting. It was a male voice.

"I am all right, Sir."

"There are not many people about at this hour. What, pray tell, has you out so late?"

"I was with friends, and now I'm going home. Why do you ask?"

"Just curious. I've been waiting for someone to pass by."

"Looking for someone to have a go with, then?"

He nodded and stepped from the doorway. He was wearing a hat that was tilted over his eyes, and a long coat. As he approached her, he came into the dim light given off from the street lamp. She saw that he was of shabby-genteel appearance.

She took hold of his hands and sniffed the air.

"Is something wrong?" he asked.

"Not at all. I like your cologne," she commented. "Nice, floral scent."

"Thank you, my dear. Shall we go now?"

"If you'd like. I know a good spot. I'll take you there."

"As you wish."

Annie smiled and put an arm around his waist. "Let's go, then, Love. I'll take care of you."

She stumbled on the uneven sidewalk.

"Easy now," the man said. "Seems like you've had a bit to drink tonight. Come on. I'll hold you while we walk. Just tell me which way to go."

Annie released him, and he put his arm around her waist. Holding her up, they walked to a semi-secluded location not far from where they had met. There was a boundary fence with a walkway between the tenement buildings. She led him there, began to show him some affection, but stopped.

"What's wrong?" he asked.

"I'm sorry, Love, but with all the drink, I have to pee."

"Oh?"

"You'll stay right here and wait for me, won't you, Love? I'll just go up the walk a little further, take care of myself and then come back, all right?"

"Yes, that's fine."

"Thank you, Love," Annie said, as she kissed him.

She walked about ten yards along the fence, and kept her back to the man. She moved her clothing to prepare, squatted and proceeded to relieve herself. When she finished, she stood and rearranged her clothing. She turned with the intent to return to the man, but was startled to see that he had walked up to her location.

"I thought you were going to wait for me back there."

"No matter," he responded, "we can take care of things right here."

"If that is what you want."

"Yes it is," he replied, as he lifted his arm.

Annie saw a long, metallic object dimly reflected against the meager light.

"No!" she cried, as she was thrown against the fence.

VIII.

Arriving at the cottage just before dawn, Johnstone and Potter had time for just a brief, but somewhat energizing sleep. They rose and had breakfast in their usual fashion.

"What's the matter?" Johnstone asked, as he noticed Potter picking at his food.

"I was thinking of the creature we saw in the alley last night. I believe we are in serious trouble."

"Come now, how can we be in trouble?"

"I don't mean 'we' as in you and me. I mean everyone living in and around London. Anyone can fall prey to it."

"With a little care, everyone will be safe."

"I beg to differ with you," Potter argued. "That thing is among us. It is of the undead and must feed on the blood of the living in order to survive!"

"I have heard of the legends and stories."

"The legend is here today. We must destroy it before it destroys us!"

"How do you propose we do that, and why is it here to begin with? What does it want?"

"I don't know. Maybe it's looking for new feeding or to start a new brood. I admit that it will not be an easy task to destroy it. We most certainly will not be able to kill it at night. It's much too strong, and has very few weaknesses when awake. We must find where it rests during the day."

"But how could such a thing have come here?"

"These beings have many means to make their way. Perhaps this one came across the channel on one of the many ships that call on the docks near Whitechapel."

"Hmm," Johnstone thought. "I remember that I felt something in the fog that first night in Whitechapel when we encountered it. The fog stopped and drifted all around us before continuing to the alley."

"That was the creature. It lives in the fog. It exuded the smell of lilac. Such a pleasant aroma, but behind it is death!"

"But we've only seen the man, the blue fog and a bat thus far. How could this being live in the fog? If so, where does it go?"

"The legends are many, and the forms these beings take likewise. If this one lives in the fog, I don't know how we can destroy it, but there must be a way, and we have to figure it out!"

Johnstone thought, "I hope that Miss Karanova will be all right, and the doctor is wrong about her chances."

"She'd better survive, or else she'll become like that creature, and then there will be two here feeding on the people. We'll have to destroy them both! If we don't, the two will become four, then eight..."

"I understand, Potter. How do we know there aren't more of them out there now?"

"I don't think there are."

"Why are you so sure?"

"There haven't been any other reports about such things. This one appears only to be feeding on one person, our Miss Karanova. There is a purpose to its presence, and to what it's doing. But what is it? If we can figure that out, we can probably find its weakness."

"What of the murders in Whitechapel? Maybe after it feeds, it stalks and kills?"

"I don't know. Unfortunately, I don't believe that there are many experts on these things."

"You're probably correct on that." Johnstone finished his breakfast. "Are you going to eat anything?" he asked.

"No. I haven't much of an appetite this morning. I am more concerned with the events at hand, and how Miss Karanova has fared."

"I for one, hope to God that she did not die. Such a lovely young woman. What of her child if she did die?" Johnstone wiped his mouth with a napkin. "Very well. Let's clean up as fast as we can, and get to the hospital so we can speak with Colonel Morrison."

When they arrived at the hospital, Morrison had already been waiting outside for a considerable amount of time. They noticed that he was in an excited state. Before their carriage even stopped, he ran up to it and opened the door.

"It's about time you got back!" he spoke in a fast manner.

"Good morning to you, too, Thomas! What is the word on Miss Karanova?" asked Johnstone.

Morrison caught himself and calmed down a bit. "Yes, my apologies. Good morning to you, William. You too, Potter."

"Sir," Potter acknowledged the greeting.

The two men got out of the carriage and walked with Morrison into the hospital.

Morrison now responded to Johnstone's question, and spoke at a slower pace, "The doctor says that Miss Karanova is extremely weak, but she should pull through. He doesn't know how that could be possible, considering her condition when we brought her in here last night. She lost so much blood that they gave her a transfusion. She is a strong, young woman, and she will recover. However, the doctor says it'll take several weeks of rest, maybe even a month or more."

"Thank God!" Johnstone exclaimed.

"Now," continued Morrison, "did you hear the other news?"

"What news?"

"There was another murder last night."

"Another one in Whitechapel?" Potter asked. "When?"

"The victim was found about six this morning in Spitalfields. She was cut up pretty badly, I understand."

"After we chased that thing away from us, he went and killed," remarked Johnstone. "This murder is our fault. He said that he was going to taste more British blood. Damn, we had him and we let him go!"

"I gave the police the information about our friend," Morrison reported. "They'll be on the watch for him now."

"Good!" exclaimed Johnstone.

"There's one more thing," Morrison said.

"What's that?"

"The victim was Annie, one of the women who came up to our table in the public house the other night."

"Yes, I remember her," Johnstone shook his head.

As they talked in the hallway, a doctor left the ward where Violetta was being kept. He recognized Morrison and informed him that Violetta was awake. The doctor permitted the men to see her, but cautioned them that she was in a very fragile state. They entered the ward. The walls were painted a drab green. There were no wall hangings or other decorations present to break up the septic appearance of the room. The ward was sparsely furnished, containing twelve patient beds and a few chairs. Only half of the beds were in use. A nurse led them to the bed where Violetta lay.

"Good morning, Miss Karanova," greeted Johnstone.

She held up her left hand. Johnstone grasped it lightly in his. She looked very weak, but managed to give a small smile to her benefactors. Despite her appearance, the others returned a smile.

"You men help me so much."

"It's nothing," replied Johnstone.

"Yes, you help so much. I make big trouble for you. I sorry for being trouble."

"Nonsense!" offered Morrison. "We only wanted to help you."

"Yes. I know."

"How are you feeling?" Johnstone asked.

"I feel good soon. Then I go and must work. Daughter need food."

To the surprise of the others, Johnstone suddenly offered to take her to his cottage when she was strong enough to leave the hospital. She would be able to remain there to rest as long as needed to regain her health, he told her. She politely declined his offer, citing the need to take care of her child. Johnstone tactfully countered her argument, and she was forced to acknowledge that in her present condition she would not be able to provide proper care to her daughter anyway. With Johnstone's persuasion, she finally agreed and relented, but requested that they first go to her tenement to inform her mother of Johnstone's offer. She wanted to see her mother and child to let them know what had happened and what she realized she needed to do to get well. She would also have the chance to gather the personal effects and clothing she would need during her convalescent stay with Johnstone.

The next morning, Violetta was released from the hospital. Johnstone and Morrison came to help transport her home. Potter had remained at the cottage to prepare it for her arrival.

Her mother was suspicious of the men's intentions, but Violetta voiced her confidence in them. Johnstone also mentioned that Violetta would be able to get better care with him, as he would engage his personal doctor to look after her. The hospital, and certainly Whitechapel, could not offer the same medical attention. Johnstone offered some money to help with the child's needs while Violetta was convalescing at his cottage.

Violetta's mother had concerns about three strange men offering to take her daughter outside of London. However, she saw her daughter's weakness and knew that if she tried to dissuade Violetta, it could make things worse. Reluctantly, she agreed to the arrangement.

Violetta's mother, with Morrison and Johnstone helping, packed what Violetta needed. After a tearful farewell exchange with her three-year-old daughter, Violetta was carefully placed in

Johnstone's carriage and transported to the cottage. Potter had everything prepared by the time they arrived. Violetta was given Johnstone's bedroom, and Potter agreed to watch over her and take care of her daily needs. Johnstone had communicated with his personal doctor and instructed him to make no less than daily visits to check on Violetta's recovery.

The doctor was present as they put Violetta to bed. He checked her condition and concurred that she had been very lucky to have survived. "I can see that you're a strong young woman, Miss Karanova," the doctor told her, "but I think that your recovery will take at least two months before you will be able to return home. If you go any sooner, you will be seriously risking your health."

Violetta was obviously disappointed by the instructions from the doctor, but nodded nonetheless.

The doctor saw her reaction and said, "Now, Miss Karanova, it won't be all that bad. You will be able to get out of bed soon. Maybe in two weeks you'll be strong enough to walk about, and stay up a little longer each day. Don't worry. Everything will be fine. You'll see. Follow my instructions, and you'll be able to go home soon. How does that sound to you?"

This time Violetta returned a smile, and said, "I do as you say, doctor. Thank you for take care of me."

"You're quite welcome, me dear. Now you rest, and I'll be back tomorrow."

The doctor gathered his medical bag and prepared to leave. Johnstone followed him outside.

"Colonel, she is a bright, young woman. It's hard to believe what she does for a living."

"Doctor," Johnstone replied, "life seems to give most people bad turns, especially if they do not have sufficient means to take care of themselves financially. She got with a no-good husband, and now has to take care of her life and family the best way she can."

The doctor sighed as he stepped into his carriage. "That's all very much a sad truth. However, it certainly used to be much worse than it is today. Thank God the Queen has an interest in helping the poor. She has done so much for them."

"Yes, she has, God save her, but after seeing how things are in Whitechapel, there is so much more to do."

"I will see you tomorrow then, and check up on my new patient."

The doctor left and Johnstone returned to the cottage.

"William," Morrison said as Johnstone entered, "I believe I shall take my leave of you. We all need to get a good rest."

"Yes, I certainly agree with you on that, Thomas!"

"With the murder last night, what do you say we give the police a chance to do their work, and we go down to Scotland Yard in, say, about a week's time and find out the status of the investigation?"

"That will be fine. It'll give Potter and me time to care for Miss Karanova. The first couple of weeks will probably be the most critical for her anyway. She will need much attention until then."

IX.

Despite his instructions to Potter to see to Violetta's daily needs, Johnstone spent most of the first week tending to her. The young woman's body worked hard to replenish its strength, but as Johnstone watched, he knew that Violetta's recovery would take a long time. He sat with her when she was awake, although those periods for the first week were very short. He repositioned her in the bed when she was uncomfortable, and he even took care of her bedpan. She was too weak to converse with him, and most of the tending was done in silence.

One day a soft knock was heard at the door. It was Colonel Morrison. He met briefly with Potter and Johnstone, and even looked in to see how Violetta was doing. He was surprised to see so little change in her condition. However, Morrison's purpose for his visit was to pick up Johnstone. Potter was left to take care of Violetta while the others rode to London for a meeting with Sir Charles.

***

"I just don't understand it, Sir Charles," Morrison stated when the briefing was concluded. "The man we saw is easily identified by his attire compared with that of those who live in the district. He also speaks with an Eastern European accent, and uses lilac cologne."

"Colonel Morrison," Sir Charles replied, "we have had no one come forward to identify your suspect as the one wanted for the murders. No one that we have talked to recollects even seeing this man, except you and your companions. Your best witness, as you tell me, can't remember even being with him!"

Morrison protested, "But we have seen him several times, and my continued investigation at the hospital shows that there have now been other women admitted in a similar condition to Miss Karanova's."

Sir Charles looked through a stack of papers on his desk. "I do not doubt what you have seen and what you have discovered, but what you describe does not match with what we've been told by witnesses."

"What do you mean, Sir Charles?" Johnstone asked.

"Until last week's murder, no one had been able to give us a description of the suspect. Now, we believe that we have a good description from someone who saw the last victim shortly before she was murdered." He found the paper he was looking for, and continued, "We found a witness who was in the area shortly before this Annie Chapman was murdered. The witness stated that Chapman was with a dark-haired man of 'shabby-genteel appearance'."

"Hmm," said Morrison.

"That is a direct quotation from the witness. Now that doesn't sound like your man at all, I'm sorry to say."

"Was there any mention of any fog at that time by your witness?" Morrison asked.

"Yes. There was a report of a small patch of blue fog in the area. It was probably a blue color due to the reflection of a nearby light.That would not have any effect on the witness's statement, however."

"No, it wouldn't," agreed Johnstone, "but maybe our suspect was wearing different clothing. In addition, this man has the power to put people into a trance. They can't remember much of their encounters with him. Thomas was put under his control."

"Is that true? How did this happen?"

"Sir Charles," Morrison responded, "I remember seeing the blue fog. We watched it as it went into an alley. We followed it, and then saw our suspect come out of that same alley. There was no fog to be seen when we got there. Just that man. He made contact with Miss Karanova and they went into another alley near the Ten Bells Public House. We saw this happen on different nights. It always unfolded in the same manner.

"On the night that we tried to confront him, I remember seeing his eyes glowing bright red like they were on fire. He looked at me, and I could feel his glaze pierce through me like a bullet. I can't say anything else about my encounter with him, because I don't remember anything about it. It was like I was asleep, and then I awoke and William was talking to me as I lay on the street."

"And where was your suspect?" asked Sir Charles.

"He had gone; left the scene," Johnstone answered.

Earlier, while enroute to the meeting, the two men had agreed that they did not want to bring up all of the events that had occurred that night, especially the possibility of vampirism. They thought that would not be well received by Sir Charles, and could jeopardize his confidence in their work.

"Well, gentlemen, I can offer you this," Sir Charles began, in an obvious move to signal the end of the meeting. "We will keep on the watch for your suspect, and we will talk to him if we find him. Up to this point I can tell you that none of my men has reported seeing any blue fog in Whitechapel or on the river. Of course, their instructions are to look for a murderer, not fog." He sighed and then said, "And no one has seen any man fitting your description, but it could be that we haven't found those witnesses yet. However, as I have said, we will watch for him."

"I guess there is always the possibility," added Johnstone, "that the man we have seen could be an accomplice, or maybe there is more than one murderer out there."

"That is always a possibility," agreed Sir Charles. "That is why he is of interest to us, and why we will talk to him when we get the opportunity."

"I suppose that will be all we can hope for," lamented Morrison.

"Colonel Morrison, don't discount the work that you and your friends have done for us. You have been and continue to be a big help in this investigation. We still, however, need more information. Let's see what else you can find out there in Whitechapel." Sir Charles stood, and the others with him. "You keep conducting your surveillance and letting us know what you see and hear."

X.

The need for the men to resume their work in the East End conflicted with Violetta's pressing need for care. Potter stated that he would stay with her while Johnstone and Morrison resumed their task. Johnstone still spent many hours during the day tending to her needs. He tried to rest during the times that she was asleep. The surveillance work and tending to Violetta was taking a physical toll on Johnstone, but he insisted on spending the time on both tasks.

Morrison and Johnstone decided to venture into other areas of Whitechapel in an attempt to find and talk to people who did not frequent the High Street area. Although deemed necessary to obtain information, this effort brought the two into some of the most dangerous portions of the district in terms of both safety and health. Morrison, unknown to Johnstone, began to carry a small pistol for protection.

The police, on their own, and with the additional reports provided by Johnstone and Morrison, were able to take several men into custody for questioning. Johnstone and Morrison's prime suspect, however, was not among those detained.

As the second half of September continued, and autumn became the official season, the weather became decidedly worse. A cold, damp and thick gray fog became a nightly shroud blanketing all of London. Reports of a blue fog intermixed with the gray became more widespread. Try as Johnstone and Morrison did to intercept the blue fog, it continued to elude them.

In an attempt to increase their eyes and ears for the surveillance, the two made contact with George Lusk, who was the president of the Whitechapel Vigilance Committee. They agreed to share information, and to meet weekly to plan strategies for more in-depth surveillance to permit them to cover more area in the East End. This proved helpful to both volunteer groups, but it did not lead Johnstone and Morrison any closer to the blue fog.

They made checks of the hospitals in the East End, but found no further occurrences of women brought in for symptoms similar to Violetta's. It was as if the fog and the being within it had vanished.

One evening, the three men were having dinner at the cottage. Their discussion about the latest news on the investigation served to update Potter, who was spending the nights watching over Violetta.

"So," Johnstone said, "we are at a loss as to what happened to the fog and our friend."

Potter offered a conjecture that the being may have changed feeding tactics. The others questioned the validity of his statement.

"Well," Potter replied, "remember that this being is not an animal, whatever his actions may seem like. He was a human being once, and therefore has the intelligence that he had from the time he lived as a human."

The two nodded acceptance of that fact.

Potter continued, "The being has seen us several times. He knows that we are trying to track him. It only makes sense that he would change what he is doing to keep us off his trail."

The two agreed with this as well.

"So, doesn't it make sense that instead of feeding on just one woman and almost draining her of her life, he might begin feeding on many? This way no one would be as drained as Miss Karanova was, and the new feeding stock would not have a need to go to hospital and raise suspicion."

"Now that makes total sense to me," Johnstone said. "What do you think, Thomas?"

He nodded, "Yet, won't everyone whom he's feeding on become like him?"

"Only if he kills them by sucking the life force from them, meaning taking all of their blood so that death ensues as a result."

"So, he has probably established feeding stock of God knows how many!" Morrison exclaimed. "We can't go about the entire East End looking at everyone's neck! Besides, with the colder weather upon us, people are bundled in heavier clothing making it even harder to observe."

"There might be another problem," Potter interjected.

"What's that?" asked Johnstone.

"If he begins to feel threatened, he may sire one or more of his kind to protect him from us. It could act as a decoy or a guard."

The two sat and looked at Potter.

"Do you know what you're saying, Potter?" Morrison asked. "If he does that with people from the East End...well, they are not the most educated people around. Many act almost like animals now. If they become like him, it will be an utter nightmare for the East End and probably all of London!"

Johnstone sneezed.

"Bless you, William," offered Morrison.

"Thank you," Johnstone said, as he sneezed again.

Their aggressive work in the East End and taking care of Violetta had taken its toll, and he had succumbed to a severe cold. With Johnstone now ill, they decided to suspend their work until he was better.

XI.

The doctor now had two patients to care for. Potter gave up his bed to Johnstone, as Violetta was still too weak to leave the bed she was using, although she was showing some signs of improvement.

On one of his daily visits, the doctor was rubbing some ointment on Johnstone's chest. "I think it would do you well to stay in bed as much as possible for a fortnight at least. You are quite physically drained, which is what probably made it easy for you to get sick like this."

"The way I feel right now, Doctor, I have no argument for you."

"All right, now button up your shirt and start taking better care of yourself."

"But I want to take care of her to make sure that she gets well."

"Potter can handle that task for the time being." The doctor instructed, as he looked at Johnstone.

"What is it?" the Johnstone asked.

"Just an observation, my friend…I understand you want the best for Miss Karanova. I don't know if there is anything more than that."

"I don't know either, Doctor. Why are you bringing this up?"

"Well, I don't intend to sound cruel, but you must remember her status and where she comes from. One has to be careful about what he is seeing. It can be hard to tell."

"Tell what?"

"To be able to tell whether the woman in question is a damsel in distress, or just a distressed damsel. Time will reveal the answer. One must be mindful not to jump to a conclusion regarding this too early."

"I will keep that thought in mind, Doctor."

The doctor left for the day. Johnstone lay on the bed thinking about what he had been told. He closed his eyes and saw Violetta's face. Although in her current physical condition it did not happen too often, he could envision her infectious smile and giggle. He thought of their short talks in both Russian and English. He smiled and felt a warm glow in his heart. This was a feeling that, until recently, was foreign to him.

XII.

Late in the afternoon of the following Saturday, there came a pounding on the front door of the cottage. Potter was irritated at the sudden noise. He quickly ran to the door and opened it. He was about to reprimand the visitor when Morrison rushed into the room.

"William!" Morrison yelled excitedly, and started towards Johnstone's bedroom.

"Colonel, please!" Potter stated as loudly as possible while still maintaining the semblance of a whisper.

Morrison caught himself and addressed Potter in a much lower tone, "Oh dear, Potter. I'm dreadfully sorry for the disturbance."

"That is all right, Sir," Potter responded.

"I must speak with Colonel Johnstone," Morrison said, and started once again towards Johnstone's bedroom.

"Colonel," Potter called.

"Yes?"

"Colonel Johnstone is in my room for the time being."

Morrison looked towards Johnstone's bedroom and said, "Yes, of course. I forgot. Thank you, Potter."

Morrison started towards the other bedroom, but Johnstone had been aroused by the commotion, and entered the front room. Johnstone was in his pajamas and house robe. He looked tired, but his cold was waning.

"I'm terribly sorry to have brought you out of bed, William, but something's come up and I had to see you."

Johnstone sneezed and blew his nose.

"Oh dear, William, maybe I should have postponed coming over here another day or two."

"Thomas, it'll be all right. You're here, so let's get on with it, shall we?"

"Do you feel well enough to talk to me today?"

Johnstone smiled, "I think I shall survive this day no matter what happening brought you here." He walked over to the couch and sat down.

Morrison pulled over a chair and sat in it across from Johnstone. Potter did likewise.

"All right," Johnstone said, as he sneezed a couple of times. "What brings you here today?"

"William, late this morning I was summoned to Sir Charles' office."

Johnstone perked up, "Did they…"

"No," Morrison interrupted, "unfortunately not. I wish to God that they had. However, when I arrived, Sir Charles showed me a piece of paper that he had received from the Central News Agency."

"A piece of paper?"

"Well, a letter actually. Sir Charles let me read it. I transcribed it verbatim and rushed over here directly after my meeting to share this with you."

Morrison handed the paper to Johnstone who began to read it.

"*Dear Boss*?"

"That's how it began. I believe it refers to Sir Charles."

Johnstone resumed reading the letter. He read it mostly to himself, but he vocalized some of the sentences as he read, and commented on the poor grammar and spelling...

"I keep on hearing the police have caught me but they wont fix me just yet. I have laughed when they look so clever and talk about being on the right track. That joke about Leather Apron gave me real fits. I am down on whores and I shant quit ripping them till I do get buckled. Grand work the last job was. I gave the lady no time to squeal. How can they catch me now. I love my work and want to start again. You will soon hear of me with my funny little games. I saved some of the proper red stuff in a ginger beer bottle over the last job to write with but it went thick like glue and I cant use it. Red ink is fit enough I hope ha. ha. The next job I do I shall clip the ladys ears off and send to the police officers just for jolly wouldn't you. Keep this letter back till I do a bit more work, then give it out straight. My knife's so nice and sharp I want to get to work right away if I get a chance. Good Luck.

Yours truly,

Jack the Ripper

Dont mind me giving the trade name

PS Wasnt good enough to post this before I got all the red ink off my hands curse it No luck yet. They say I'm a doctor now. ha ha"

Johnstone handed the paper to Potter and looked at Morrison, "Jack the Ripper?"

"Yes! Contact from the murderer!"

"Good Lord!" exclaimed Potter. "This is unbelievable!"

"Yes," agreed Johnstone. "This madman is turning this into a game now! Didn't our friend make similar threats?"

"He has to be found as soon as possible," Morrison urged.

"Yes," Johnstone agreed, "he isn't going to stop now. Good Lord, how many more victims will there be before he's caught?"

"I don't know," replied Morrison, "but the sooner everyone involved with this investigation gets out and blankets the East End, the quicker he will be found!"

"Colonel Morrison, you said that this letter was received by the Central News Agency, correct?" Potter asked.

"Yes. Why, Potter?"

"Then this will end up in the papers. How will the people react to it?"

Morrison looked at Johnstone, "William, we must resume our work as quickly as possible. However, you do not look up to the task at the moment."

"You are correct, Thomas. I will do no good out there at the present. In a few days, I'll probably be recovered enough to return there. If I started now, I would probably only get worse."

Johnstone sneezed.

"Yes, best that you remain at home. I, however, intend to return to the East End and resume the work."

"Are you sure this is a wise decision, Colonel Morrison?" Potter asked.

"Don't worry. I will be careful. William, when you are well enough, have word sent to me, and we shall meet and discuss our next actions. In the meantime, I will return if I learn anything new.

XIII.

A comfortable breeze blew in the early Saturday afternoon on the twenty-ninth day of September. Taking advantage of the surprisingly good weather, Potter had opened the windows to the cottage to freshen the air inside. With his other chores completed, Potter had gone to Thurrock to obtain food and supplies.

Johnstone, feeling much better, went to his bedroom to check on Violetta. At first glance, he saw an empty bed. A slight panic set in, but he then noticed that she was sitting on a chair by the window. She was looking out, and seemed lost in thought.

"Do you need anything, Miss Karanova?" he asked, concerned that she might not be able to sit out of bed for much longer.

"Hmm?" she said softly, and then turned towards him. "Please forgive me, Colonel. I was looking out window at river and was dreaming."

"That's quite all right, Miss Karanova. There's no need for you to apologize."

"Thank you for being so good to me. You a great man."

Johnstone was embarrassed by the compliment, "Thank you, but I'm no one special."

"Hmm," Violetta responded in a contrary tone.

"Well," Johnstone wanted to change the subject, "I must say that this is the best you've looked since you arrived."

"How is the Colonel Johnstone feeling?" she smiled.

Now that Violetta was beginning to look better, her smile was even more infectious, and Johnstone could not help but smile back at her. "The Colonel is feeling much better, thank you."

"That is good. You such a caring man. I hated to see you not well."

"I believe this warmer turn in the weather is helpful to both of us."

"Hmm," her voice broke as she turned back to the window. "I miss my little girl."

Johnstone saw a tear roll down her face.

She lamented, "It such a lovely day. I would be in lovely garden or park playing with her if I lived in Moscow. No garden or park to play here in England where I live."

"I'm sorry," Johnstone spoke in a consoling tone.

"It not your fault. You and other men saved my life. I probably be dead now if you not find me. My daughter would then have no mother." She abruptly changed the conversation, "I hear you men talking."

"I apologize if our discussions have been disturbing to you."

"No, it not that. Damn!"

"What is it?" Johnstone asked, surprised at Violetta's swearing.

"It bad enough women have to do what we do to take care of family. Now, someone kill us!"

"I'll make sure in the future that we discuss this outside or someplace else, so we don't disturb you. You should not listen to us. You need to rest peacefully."

Johnstone watched her as she resumed gazing out the window.

"Miss Karanova, do you feel well enough to see your daughter?"

She quickly turned towards him, almost falling out of the chair as a result. Johnstone moved towards her, but she recovered and balanced herself in the chair.

"Colonel, can you bring her to me?"

"If you feel up to it, I'll do just that. I don't have a park here, but my land is well kept like a garden around the cottage. She can play here as long as she wants."

Violetta stood and slowly took the few steps needed to reach him. She put her arms around him in a hug. "Thank you," she cried.

Johnstone broke the hug and gave her a handkerchief.

She wiped her eyes. "You know, Colonel, sometimes when you in dirt all day and night, you forget there are nice things and nice people out there."

"I'm just..." Johnstone choked up and broke off what he started to say. He gathered himself, and continued, "I'll go and bring your daughter here tomorrow."

"Thank you so much," Violetta responded, her demeanor transformed with joy.

She walked back to the chair, sat down and resumed looking out the window. A breeze came through and her long, soft hair gently waved in it. Johnstone started to leave the room when he heard her begin to hum a Russian lullaby. He stopped outside the doorway to listen. It made him feel warm inside and he shed a couple of tears in response.

XIV.

That evening, a determined Colonel Morrison went alone to Whitechapel. The pleasant weather, a distinct change from the previous week of cold and rain, brought a larger than normal crowd in the area, even for a Saturday night.

The *Dear Boss* letter angered him and he was more resolved than ever to find the fiend who identified himself as "Jack the Ripper". He went to the riverbank and looked out towards the river as the evening turned to night. He watched and waited for any sign of the blue fog.

While he waited, his thoughts fixated on the letter and some of the phrases contained in it. *"I shant quit ripping them..."* echoed in his mind. He had viewed police photographs and attended coroner inquests of the murdered women. The views of the brutality of the acts flashed in his mind. He could not reconcile how someone could be so vicious towards another. In his mind, it could only be something sub-human. He recounted how Violetta was attacked and how the three had rescued her. He was certain now that what he was pursuing, the suspect in these unsolved criminal acts, existed in the blue fog.

The night continued. The church bells struck the time. It was now ten o'clock. There was still no sign of the fog. Colonel Morrison was becoming impatient, and began pacing along the shore. His fixation on the letter continued. He could not get the words and phrases out of his mind, *"...shant quit ripping them..."*; *"...I love my work..."*; *"funny little games..."*; *"...my knife's so nice and sharp...*". He even superimposed the accented voice of the being they encountered onto the words. Repeatedly, he imagined hearing the being speaking the phrases from the letter. Then the ending of the letter with its "*ha ha*" and it repeated "*ha ha*" as it continuously repeated getting louder in his mind with each iteration, "*ha ha...HA HA... HA HA... HA HA!*"

Morrison put his hands over his ears, and shouted, "Stop it! God in heaven, stop it!"

A tall, slender woman and her boyfriend of the moment were walking on a worn path along the shore and approaching Morrison at the time of his outburst. They had been looking for a quiet location where she could show her appreciation for his "donation" to her.

Hearing Morrison shouting, the man said to his companion, "Come on, Lizzie. We'd best quickly move on from here."

She agreed and they turned from Morrison as they took a fast-paced walk away from him. As they retreated, they looked back several times to see if he was following them. He had not moved, but was watching them, and recognized Lizzie from the pub where they had taken Violetta. Morrison was embarrassed at having had such an outburst in public. The interruption served to chase the demons from his mind.

After distancing themselves from Morrison, and seeing that he did not intend to chase after them, the couple resumed a normal walking pace. A short moment later, with Morrison still watching, Lizzie stopped and pointed out towards the river. He likewise looked out to try to see at what the woman was pointing.

"Yes!" he exclaimed in a loud voice that echoed through the area. "At last! Come ashore, you devil! I will take you down tonight!"

The couple, hearing this new outburst, started to run from the area.

"Stay away from the blue fog!" Morrison yelled after them.

Morrison ran down the riverbank to where Lizzie had been standing. Above the water, a fog bank was forming. A faint blue shimmering was emanating from within it. As the size of the fog bank increased, so did the brightness of the blue hue. It continued to grow, and began a swirling motion. It started moving towards the shore as soon as a clock tower in the district struck midnight. The fact that it was now Sunday did nothing to dissuade the blue fog from its approach.

Morrison saw that it would come ashore down river from where he stood. Not wanting to waste any further time watching the event, he started towards the location where he believed the fog would come ashore. He ran along the riverbank as far as he could in order to keep the fog in his sight. He carefully watched for any change in the fog's movement and direction of travel. After following the riverbank as far as possible, the path became too treacherous to continue in the night without endangering his safety. He stopped near Tower Bridge and saw the fog coming ashore. However, he lost sight of it as it passed behind the Tower of London. He turned and ran northward towards Whitechapel on the street that led away from the bridge.

He reached High Street, but no longer could see the fog. He

was becoming frantic and stopped people in the street to ask them if they had seen any fog. Most thought he had been drinking a bit too much and walked away from him. Undaunted, he continued and finally found someone who acknowledged seeing a blue fog near Dutfield's Yard. He asked directions and was told that the yard was located behind the International Working Men's' Educational Club off Berner Street. He hired a cab on Whitechapel High Street to take him to the club.

It took about fifteen minutes to reach the yard. After disembarking from the carriage, he stopped for a brief moment in front of the club in order to view the surroundings. Not wanting to delay too long, he slowly made his way to the corner of the club. He poked only a small portion of his head around the corner so that he could look into the yard without being seen. The yard was extremely dark, with nothing in the area providing any illumination. He could make out from the outline of roofs in the sky that it was a small courtyard surrounded by buildings. He was unable to see much of anything else, but believed that he heard someone moving about. He summoned his strength and entered the yard.

"You there!" Morrison challenged.

He heard footsteps that sounded as if someone were running away. Then there was the sound of someone tripping and falling to the ground. Whoever it was then struggled to rise and resumed the flight.

"I say, 'you there'! Halt!" he challenged again.

He no longer heard the footsteps, but there was a shape

standing several yards away from him on the right side of the courtyard. He started towards it, then saw two red glowing circles about six feet off the ground. The circles focused on him, turning a darker shade of red. They then began to glow slightly brighter. Morrison stopped his approach as he felt a piercing through his eyes and knew that he had found the being that he was looking for. He remembered Potter's instructions to avoid looking into its eyes.

Hearing a groan, Morrison diverted his eyes downward towards the ground. He saw what looked to be a body lying there. Another groan came from it. He knelt beside it, and could see that the victim was female. The being's eyes caused an eerie illumination of the woman, which enabled Morrison to see blood gushing in spurts from a wound on her throat. He could make out her face; it was Lizzie.

He stood, and defiantly faced the being. "This all ends here, tonight! You shall not continue your morbid games any longer!" Morrison commanded.

Morrison moved again towards the woman, but the being stepped towards him.

"You will stand aside and let me help her!"

The being growled and spoke in a deep, threatening, but quiet voice, "There is no hope for her. You will leave this place now!"

"I think not!" Morrison responded defiantly, still avoiding eye contact.

"I warned you and your comrades to stay out from underfoot. You know not what you are interfering with. I give you one last warning."

The *clip...clop* of hooves and the squeaking of the wheels of a cart became audible as a pony and cart turned into the yard. Morrison turned towards the street.

"Now, we shall take care of business," Morrison stated as he produced his pistol and turned back towards the being.

It was no longer there.

"Who's there?" called the cart driver.

Morrison did not want to become involved in the police investigation of the scene, and thought it better to pursue the being. He did not respond to the call, figuring that the driver would find the woman and alert the police. Morrison ran out the back of the right side of the yard into an alley. He believed that it was the only direction in which the being could have fled.

As he left the yard, Morrison turned to look back. Through the open steps of a staircase, he saw that the cart driver had lit a match and had found the woman. The driver began calling loudly for the police. Morrison resumed his pursuit. Back in the yard, a police whistle sounded.

Morrison found himself on Commercial Street and ran westward. When he reached the Aldgate area, he had to stop to catch his breath. On the way to his present location, he did not spot any sign of the being, and knew that he had lost him again. Breathing heavily, he looked about his surroundings. There were still a good number of people walking about in the area. Then, he heard the sound of another police whistle.

A constable answering his colleague's call came running and passed by Morrison.

"Stand clear! Make way!" the constable yelled as he made his way up the street.

People came running from the direction to which the constable was heading. Morrison overheard talk about a woman being found murdered in Mitre Square just two blocks from where Morrison was standing. Some of the people started towards the square in an attempt to satisfy their morbid curiosity. He heard a few of the people in the crowd talking about a murder in Dutfield's Yard.

The news of two murders in such close proximity to each other sent many in the area into a small panic. Speculation began that the murderer was probably still in the area. Those who did not venture towards the square made haste to return to their homes or sought refuge with others in the friendly confines of a pub.

Surveying the scene, Morrison concluded that the suspect, if he was still in the area, would be unable to escape to the south. That was the location where the police and onlookers were gathering. He decided to approach the square by going around to the north side where it appeared that most people were not headed. He took a deep breath and resumed his pursuit.

He ran one block and then turned north onto Dukes's Place. At the next corner was another street that would take him to the square. He turned the corner, and in doing so was almost knocked to the ground by a man who was running in the opposite direction. Morrison regained his balance and started again towards the square, only to run into someone else.

"Damn!" he exclaimed as he fell to the sidewalk. "I'm terribly sorry…"

He started to apologize when he felt a pair of strong hands grasp both of his shoulders near his neck and pick him up. He struggled, but the grip was too strong for him to break loose. He was carried, almost by the neck, to the doorway of the nearest building.

He was breathing heavily from running as much as he had. "Let go of me this instant!" he demanded, as he looked at the face of the one holding him.

He saw a pair of glaring red eyes looking directly at him. Morrison recognized the being and began to struggle, but his efforts of resistance were futile against the being's superior strength.

"You have interfered with me and my calling for the last time!" the being exclaimed in his deep voice.

"No!" Morrison responded breathlessly. "It is you who have interfered with us for the last time!"

"I think not, my friend," the being replied and tightened his grip on Morrison. "I will answer my calling. It is why I exist. It is why I am here!"

Morrison tried to produce the pistol from his coat pocket. He fumbled, and it fell to the sidewalk. Unable to attempt to retrieve it, he began to call out for help, but there was no one in the area. Either the news of the murders had chased everyone away, or they were at the crime scene in the square. He tried to struggle again and shout, but stopped in mid-sentence as he inadvertently made eye contact with the being for too long. He was brought under its control.

"I would have let you be, but your interference can no longer be tolerated. You are mine now!" the being exclaimed. He drove his elongated incisors into Morrison's neck and expertly removed his blood without spilling one drop.

The act done, the being released Morrison's body. The body fell in a heap in the doorway. The being looked about the area to see if anyone was present who could have seen his actions. No one else was there. He then transformed himself into a bat and flew off in the direction of the river, where a gray fog bank was forming. The bat flew into it and disappeared. From within the gray fog could be seen flashes of blue lightning.

XV.

A breeze and a crisp, sunny fall morning on the last day of September pushed the remnants of the previous night into memory for those who had lived through it.

Johnstone rose to the aroma of Potter's Sunday breakfast. Entering the kitchen, he was greeted by his loyal aide and friend.

"Good morning. You're looking much better today, if I may say so."

"Good morning, to you! I do indeed feel much better today; more like my normal self again!"

"Breakfast is almost ready."

"And for a change I have a hearty appetite this morning!"

"Good morning, my fine men," Violetta greeted, announcing her entrance into the kitchen.

Johnstone and Potter acknowledged her presence.

"Miss Karanova," Johnstone said, "it's certainly a pleasure to see you getting around better and better each day. I think, too, that your smile has been getting more and more beautiful as you have been recovering."

Violetta blushed, "Yes, Colonel. With your care and kindness, I feeling much stronger. You too, Mr. Potter, are good man."

Potter bowed slightly, "You are too kind, Miss Karanova," he said. "Now, would you both care to sit down to breakfast?" he invited.

The two sat at the table and waited while Potter served their meals. He then served himself and sat down as they all began to eat.

A loud pounding came from the front door, the suddenness of which startled the three.

"Good Lord!" exclaimed Potter. "Who the devil could that be?"

Potter rose from the table and went to the front room. He opened the door and a constable rushed into the room.

"I must see Colonel Johnstone immediately!" the constable declared.

"I am Colonel Johnstone," he stated, entering the room as Potter answered the door. "What can I do for you, Constable?"

"Sir," the constable began, "I have an urgent letter for you from Sir Charles."

The constable produced an envelope from his coat pocket and handed it to Johnstone.

"Thank you," Johnstone acknowledged as he began to open the envelope. "Did Sir Charles give you any special instructions?"

"No, Sir. My only instruction was to deliver this to you with all due speed. I have done so, and must now take my leave, Colonel."

"Yes, certainly. Thank you, Constable. Potter will see you out."

"Thank you, Sir," the constable replied, as Potter showed him out the door.

Potter shut the door and returned to the kitchen where Violetta had remained.

Now alone in the front room, Johnstone sat at the desk and opened the envelope. He removed the letter, unfolded the paper and began to read it. His heart sank and he felt faint upon reading the report on Morrison's death. He was shocked to read the information on the two new murders. He called for Potter; Violetta accompanied him to the room. Johnstone tried to get her to go to the bedroom, but she refused. Grudgingly, Johnstone briefly informed them of the communication. Violetta's skin lost most of its pinkish hue, and she visibly weakened when she heard the news. Johnstone escorted her to her bed.

"This is terrible," she lamented as she slipped under the bed sheets.

"Miss Karanova, I know I promised you that I would bring your daughter here today. However…"

"I knew it would not be when I heard the news of Colonel Morrison."

"I'm truly sorry, but I need to go see Sir Charles, and then I need to see Colonel Morrison's family to see what I can do for them."

"I understood," a disappointed Violetta replied. "You take care of what you do."

"Miss Karanova, I will bring your daughter here just as soon as I can. I promise."

"Yes, I know you will." She rolled over to face the wall. "I trust you what you say."

Johnstone knew that she was crying. He wanted to console her, but was not sure how she would react to him if he did. He left the room, made his preparations and left for London.

XVI.

During the next week, Johnstone attended police briefings and coroner inquests relating to the two slain women and Colonel Morrison. Newspaper reporters packed the police briefing rooms as the mass murders became the first globally reported news event of its kind. The whole of London and the surrounding area was traumatized by the details of the vicious events being reported.

Both the Metropolitan and London police forces stepped up efforts to try to apprehend the murderer. However, while many were detained and questioned, no one was charged with the crimes. The terror being felt by the populace was compounded by newspaper reports criticizing the inability of the police to find the suspect. Even newspaper accounts as far away as the United States considered the police investigation to be inept.

Coroner reports of the deaths of the two women stated similarities in methods to that of the women who had been slain previously. The coroner's report on Morrison, coupled with the police report, speculated that Morrison had inadvertently intercepted the killer while he was in flight from the Mitre Square murder scene. The fact that no blood was found at the scene of Morrison's death was reported, but was not found to be questionable since the same absence was noted at the scene of an earlier murder.

Violetta's condition had improved to the point that it was no longer necessary to maintain a constant vigil over her. Johnstone requested that Potter spend time with Morrison's family to help with the funeral and any other arrangements that they needed. With Johnstone attending the meetings and inquests, this often left Violetta alone at the cottage during the day.

To keep herself busy, Violetta performed many of Potter's chores. Johnstone had asked her not to exert herself and told her that it was not necessary for her to do any work around his home. She responded that she wanted to help as she could, because she did not want to feel like a beggar who was taking charity and giving nothing in return.

While there was total honesty in what she told Johnstone, she had another reason to make herself busy while she was in the cottage by herself. Violetta did all that she could to hide it from Johnstone and Potter, but she had become depressed over not being able to see her daughter. She was not quite strong enough to take a carriage ride to her home, and Johnstone and Potter were too busy to be able to arrange to bring her daughter to the cottage. She knew that soon she would be able to go home, but the anxiety caused by the separation from her daughter weighed heavily on her. As the week wore on, her loneliness grew.

Johnstone's modest estate was well kept. Potter kept the lawn close to the cottage very trim. Flowers and shrubs surrounded the cottage. The remainder of the acreage was kept mowed by a local farmer who, in exchange for the service, was permitted to recover the cut grass to feed his livestock.

As Violetta became stronger, she liked to take short walks about the property. One late afternoon, she walked down towards the river. A slight breeze was blowing from the south. Crossing the water, the air obtained a chill. As it passed, she felt the coolness and held her shawl closer to her.

She was in a contemplative state as she walked towards the riverbank. Her thoughts drifted back and forth like the gentle waves she watched brushing against the shore. There were the daydreams of what she wanted her life to be, the unpleasant vision of her current life, memories of pleasant days tending to her child, the horror that almost took her life, and Johnstone's kindness towards her.

Halfway to the river, she stopped, turned and looked back at the cottage. It sat on top of a small hill not quite fifty yards from the shore. She looked at the yard with the well-groomed shrubbery and flowers surrounding the home. A gentle plume of smoke rose from the chimney. The smoke slowly bent and twisted in an almost romantic interplay with the breeze. She took a deep breath and smiled at her personal thoughts of the sight, but she was unable to stop the tears that began to well up in her eyes.

To Violetta, the scene was pleasant and comforting in a way she had never known in her life. She envisioned children running about the yard and imagined their laughter as they played. The daydream was short. She knew her place in the social ladder, and knew that she would soon return to her own life in the East End with its noise, filth, crime and overcrowding. Still, she wished that someday she could find something simple and peaceful like what Johnstone had for himself. She turned away from the cottage and continued her slow walk to the river.

Tall reeds and grasses, waving in the breeze, lined the shore, except for a small area that was open due to a small, flat rock ledge that jutted several feet out over the water. She walked out onto the ledge, and looked to the west. She could see the capital city, where her past and future life was.

Violetta moved to the edge of the rock and looked down into the water. She saw a large number of minnows darting about her reflection. She then knelt down on the rock and looked out upon the river. The water flowed peacefully towards the sea. On this day, the river was uncommonly devoid of ships.

Closer to the water, she looked over the edge of the rock. Ripples caused minor distortions, but through it she saw the face of a young and pretty woman. She looked deep into her reflected green eyes. For the first time in her life, she saw her internal sadness and disappointment. She began to cry and watched the tears rolled down the face of her reflection. With the tears dropping from her face into the water, the actual teardrops met the reflected ones.

Her emotional state grew more despairing as she stood and looked up the river at London, and then back to look at the cottage. Revulsion came over her as thoughts of her life flooded her mind. A growing unwillingness to return to the life she knew in the East End was met with a wave of depression, and her tears became uncontrollable. She knew that her desire to remain in this peaceful place and the reality of her life in the East End were irreconcilable.

Blinded by tears, and feeling as if she was commanded to do so, she involuntarily stood, lifted and held her dress above her knees and stepped into the water. Her shoes and stockings held back the chilly water from her feet and legs for only a brief moment. She took a couple of steps away from the shore. The water became deeper. It was now up to her knees, and she let go of the dress. At first, it lifted and floated from her body like an umbrella. Then, as the cotton material absorbed the water, the ends sank and clung to her legs.

Numbness came over her as she looked through teary eyes at her dismal reflection. A small distortion appeared in the water by her reflected right shoulder. It grew larger in shape becoming clearer, though remaining blurred by the water ripples, as it did so. She saw the face of a man. Then, it looked at her and its red eyes glowed into hers. Caught unaware, she sank into a trance-like state. The face smiled at her, revealing its fangs, and toyed with her by appearing as if about to bite her neck. It backed away, only to move back closer to her neck. In her mesmerized state, she was incapable of being afraid. Then, the smile took on a more sinister look. Through the ripples and despite the distorted reflection, she saw the face turn towards her neck, its mouth opening wider. Then, in the water's reflection, she saw two arms appear from behind her and grab her at the waist.

"Do not move! I have you!"

"Hmm?" she mumbled, as she heard the words through her trance.

"Miss Karanova!"

"Who?" she reacted to hearing her named loudly called.

The voice sounded familiar as she felt herself being lifted out of the water. She fell backwards towards the rock ledge and landed on top of the one who was holding her.

"What in Heaven's name are you doing?"

"Doing...where?" she replied groggily. She slowly rolled off and looked at who was lying on the rock ledge and had cushioned her fall. "Colonel!"

"Are you all right?"

She slowly came out of the trance and started to shiver from the cold water.

"What happened to you?"

"What?" was her reply.

"What were you doing in the water?"

She sat up. Her mind was still clouded, but beginning to clear as she looked about her surroundings.

"I was in water?" she asked as she looked down and saw her wet clothing.

"Yes, what were you doing?"

She shook her head, unable to answer the question. Her shivering became more pronounced.

"Come on. Let's get you back to the cottage where you can change out of those clothes and warm up. I don't want you getting sick."

They stood and Johnstone put his coat over her as they started to the cottage.

"Thank you," she responded as she looked up at him. "Colonel, what you do here?"

"I came home early and looked for you in the cottage. You weren't there, so I thought you had taken a walk. I looked about and saw you going into the water. I ran down here as quickly as I could to get you out."

She stopped, turned and looked at the river. "There was man in river. He was behind me."

"You saw me when I came to pull you out."

"No, there was other man."

"Who?"

"I saw face, but could not see who it was with the water."

"Wait here a moment," Johnstone instructed as he walked over to the shore. He went out onto the rock ledge and gazed into the water. He shook his head and returned to her.

"There was man," she insisted.

"I didn't see anything in the water. If there was a man there, he is gone now in any event."

He held out his left hand. She took it with her right, and they turned to walk up the small hill to the cottage. He looked over at the right side of her face.

"What's this?" he commented.

"What?" she asked.

"If you would permit me, please," Johnstone requested, as he looked closer to the right side of her neck. There were two small streaks of blood. He took a handkerchief from his pocket and put it on her neck. The blood was still wet, but not running from any noticeable, fresh wound.

"Hold this on your neck," he instructed, "until we get back into the cottage."

He stopped walking and went back to the river. Violetta also stopped and watched him. He spent several minutes looking intensely into the water, but did not see anything. He then rejoined her and escorted her to the cottage.

When they entered the front room, Violetta gasped at what she saw on the couch.

"Colonel!" she exclaimed, and ran over to the couch. She knelt down in front of it and gently placed her hand on her sleeping daughter's head.

She had a large smile and tears on her face as she looked over to Johnstone. She stood, went to him and gave him a big hug and kiss.

"You such a good man," she whispered.

Johnstone looked at her and smiled. "You have such a lovely smile," he said.

"You smile pretty too," she responded.

"Miss Karanova…"

"No, my Colonel," she interrupted, "my name is Violetta."

Johnstone smiled and said, "She fell asleep on the way here. I put her on the couch while I went to look for you."

"She is so lovely, no?"

"Just like her mother."

"Why you so kind to me?"

"Miss Karanova…"

"No," she insisted, "Violetta."

"I think you should take advantage of this time and get changed before your daughter wakes up," Johnstone responded, while avoiding the question.

"Yes, you right. I go change now. You stay with Katrina in case she wakes up?"

"Yes, I will stay here."

"Thank you. I be right back."

Johnstone watched the girl while Violetta changed. He could hear her singing a Russian song as she readied to spend time with her daughter.

XVII.

Later that evening, Potter returned home to the sound of a little girl's laughter. In the front room, he saw Violetta sitting on the couch, and an animated Johnstone playing with the girl. The sight was a surprise to Potter, but one which he was glad to see.

Potter was introduced to Katrina, and then went to the kitchen to prepare supper. It was the first supper eaten in the cottage in several years that could be called a "special event".

After everyone had eaten, Johnstone and Potter cleaned the kitchen. Violetta offered to assist, but was told to go to the front room to spend time with her daughter. When the men finished their chore, Johnstone told Potter that he wanted to speak with him. He told Violetta that he was going outside to have a pipe, and would be back shortly.

The two men walked over to the carriage house where Johnstone informed Potter of the events at the river. They both concluded that the being they were looking for had sensed Violetta's presence and probably lured her into the water.

"Colonel, this is a serious development. Miss Karanova is in danger here."

Johnstone agreed.

"What are you going to do?" Potter asked.

Johnstone took a deep breath and sighed, "What I have to do to protect her."

They returned to the cottage and sat with Violetta and her daughter in the front room. Katrina was a pretty, lively three-year-old, who was overjoyed to be with her mother. Violetta played with Katrina by tickling her, singing Russian children's songs, drawing on paper and engaging in other little activities that toddlers everywhere like to do. Johnstone watched for signs of Violetta tiring. When he saw them, he stepped in to play with the little girl to give Violetta a respite. Violetta watched Johnstone as he played with her daughter, and smiled at how well he interacted with her. Finally, the little girl began to tire. Johnstone carried Katrina to the bedroom where Violetta put her to bed, and sang Russian lullabies to her until the little girl fell asleep.

Before they left the bedroom, Violetta hugged and kissed Johnstone. "Thank you so much for bringing my daughter to me. You special man."

They returned to the front room and sat down with Potter.

"Violetta," Johnstone began, "tomorrow is Colonel Morrison's funeral, and I was planning to take your daughter back home before it started."

Violetta was disappointed at hearing this, "Katrina not stay here a little longer?"

"I'm afraid not," Johnstone answered. Then his voice changed showing a sign of sadness, "I also think it best if I take you home as well."

"I knew I have to go home soon, but it nice here."

"Potter and I think it would be safer for you to go home considering what happened to you today in the river."

"I understand," she said dejectedly and stood. "I go to room now and pack things. I be ready to go home."

The two watched her walk to the bedroom and shut the door behind her. They heard her crying, and both sighed at the sound.

"Colonel," offered Potter, "I know you have feelings for Miss Karanova, but you are doing the right thing."

"I wish I was sure of that, Potter."

The next morning, the four drove in the carriage to Whitechapel. The lodging house where Violetta lived, and shared a small apartment with her mother, was located near Whitechapel High Street in one of the many mazes of alleyways that was prevalent in the area. Katrina had fallen asleep during the ride. Violetta carried her into the house, while Johnstone carried the luggage. Potter and the coachman waited outside with the carriage.

The apartment was comprised of two very small rooms. One room was for sleeping and changing. The other room was the main room for sitting, cooking and eating. The entire lodging house had one privy, which was located outside in the small back yard. The yard had an old, wooden fence around its perimeter. Many of the slats were either broken or missing.

Violetta put Katrina to bed, and joined Johnstone and her mother in the small main room. When he started to leave for the funeral, Violetta insisted on attending. Johnstone protested, but lost the argument. He waited a short time while Violetta dressed in an appropriate outfit. They then rejoined Potter outside and rode to the ceremony in the carriage.

Morrison had instructed his wife that upon his death he wanted to have a simple civilian funeral. He desired a closed casket, with only his immediate family and a few close friends invited to attend the service. Johnstone and Potter acted as pallbearers. During the procession, Johnstone commented to Potter that the casket seemed heavier than he expected it to be.

Following the internment, all attendees were invited to meet at Morrison's home. Johnstone introduced Violetta to Morrison's widow.

"My late husband lost his life trying to hunt down the man that tried to kill you…" She became emotional for a moment and then resumed, "I hope that what he did for you, and ultimately gave his life for, will not be forgotten or allowed to have been in vain." She began to cry, excused herself and went to her bedroom.

Violetta began to cry after Morrison's widow left the room. Johnstone saw this, approached her and put his hand under her chin. He gently lifted her head so that he could make eye contact with her.

"You did nothing wrong. Please do not cry anymore," he consoled her.

"I can not help it," she sobbed. "Mrs. Morrison right. No one should have die for me. I not worth that much."

Johnstone put his arms around her, "Violetta, yes, you are worth that much. To me, you are worth even more."

She looked at him. The words were comforting, but she was unsure of Johnstone's intentions, and of herself. She stopped crying, but offered no reply.

Sensing that it was time to leave the Morrison household, Johnstone asked Potter to remain behind for a few days to help Morrison's widow settle the late colonel's affairs.

Johnstone returned his attention to Violetta. "I think it is time that I take you home."

A smile appeared on her face, and she nodded quickly as Potter brought their overcoats. They prepared to leave.

"Potter," Johnstone began, "I shall see you back at the cottage in a few days, then."

"Yes," he replied, "don't worry. I'll take care of things here."

"Thank you."

Violetta went over to Potter. She gave him a kiss on the cheek and whispered to him, "You good man, Mr. Potter."

Potter blushed.

She turned and walked back to Johnstone. She looked up at him, took his arm, and said, "I ready now."

During the carriage ride to her home Johnstone initiated discussion with Violetta during which he revealed his growing affection towards her.

"I have never met anyone like you. The time we spent together, ever since we first met when you needed help, have made me feel so warm inside."

She was uneasy and concerned that Johnstone's feelings might be based more on sympathy than love.

"My sweet Colonel," she started and sighed, "I not kind of woman you should be with. I make no apology for me. I do what I do to feed family. There no work here. Too many people. If you want rescue me because you feel sorry for me, I thank you for that. You good man." She paused for a moment, but as Johnstone began to respond, she quickly resumed, "But, I am not, how the doctor say, 'damsel in distress'."

Johnstone was visibly shaken by her comment, and thought it a rejection.

"I say before I hear you men talk in cottage. Even when you outside, I still hear you."

"Violetta," he responded, "I wish there was something I could say to make you understand my feelings. I have fallen in love with you not because of what you are, but because of who you are. I don't care about the rest." He put her hand on his heart, and continued, "All my life has been spent in the Queen's Service. It was good to me, but it left me with an empty heart. Then I met you. Yes, I wanted to help you and your family. Maybe I did feel sorry for you, but that was only at the beginning. It makes me feel good to help people. I wanted to help you get better. I have loved seeing your pretty face as you got stronger and the color came back to your cheeks. Seeing that wonderful smile of yours opened my heart, and your spirit walked in and lives there now. Before I met you, there was nothing inside me. Now there is a fire. When I return home tonight, there won't be anyone there but me. I am tired of being alone. You give me energy, you give me so much, and I…"

She took her hand from his chest, and placed her fingers on his lips, "Please, no more," she said. "I understood."

They did not speak for the remainder of the trip to her home. Each had turned thoughts inward to attempt to clarify what had been said. Johnstone worried to himself that he might have said too much.

They looked out the windows on their own sides of the coach. They were in the East End. he filth, stench, smog and mass of people trying to survive surrounded them like a noose.

They arrived at Violetta's home and quietly stepped out of the carriage and into the apartment. Violetta and Johnstone sat in the small main room with her mother. There were only chairs on which to sit. These were kept at the table, as there was no other place to put them.

Violetta's mother spoke to Johnstone. She knew some English, but she spoke in Russian to him. She knew that Johnstone understood her language, and could respond to her in kind. Her mother was a little older than Johnstone, but years of hardship in both Russia and England had turned her hair prematurely gray. She held herself proud, however, and was well groomed and dressed.

"Colonel Johnstone," she began, "I would like you to stay for dinner. I was preparing the meal when you arrived. There isn't much, but it would make me happy if you would stay."

"Oh, Mrs. Karanova, thank you, but I couldn't impose on you like that."

"Nonsense!" she argued. "You have helped my daughter so much over the past weeks. Let me show you at least some appreciation for what you did for all of us. We could never repay you for all you have done, but I can do this for you."

"Mamma will not take 'no', Colonel," Violetta interjected, also speaking in her native tongue.

"Seems like I'm outnumbered, so I will accept your gracious offer. Thank you"

During the meager dinner, which was flavorful, if not filling, they continued their simple discussion. Most of the talk was trivial in nature, other than their talk about Violetta, and her recovery. Johnstone did not discuss his feelings about Violetta to her mother, however.

When they had finished, Johnstone offered to help clean, but Mrs. Karanova strongly objected to any help from him. He stood by; handing a couple of plates to Violetta when he thought her mother was not looking.

With the dinner completed and a few more minutes of talk wound down, Johnstone thanked Mrs. Karanova and bid her farewell. Violetta accompanied him outside to the carriage.

He took her hands in his. "Violetta, please think about what I said to you earlier. I really have fallen in love with you. I think about you all the time. It sounds crazy, but it's true. You have taught me how to smile again. With you I feel alive."

She gave him a hug. "My Colonel," she responded in English, "I will think of this. I say before, it not right for you to be with me. I love you too, but not as man. I love you as friend."

"Could you find it in your heart to love me as a man?"

"I not know now. I think of you all time too. Maybe I love, but I must think, and not shame you because of what I am."

"Violetta…"

"No more, please, my Colonel. We talk enough now. Let me think. Please."

"All right, if that is what you want. You know how I feel. My heart is open for you if you want it."

"Thank you for everything. I owe you so much. You great man. I love you for that."

Johnstone bent down to try to kiss her, but she turned her face away.

"Please, it time to go."

"All right," he said dejectedly.

He climbed into the carriage and instructed the coachman take him home. They waved to each other as the carriage drove away.

To Johnstone, the ride home seemed to take all night. Several times, he urged the coachman to drive faster, only to have the coachman state that he was going as fast as he could and still safely drive the carriage. This only served to make Johnstone more impatient.

After arriving at the cottage, Johnstone barked at the coachman and told him to put the carriage and horse away for the night. He then entered the cottage and slammed the door behind him. Standing in the front room, he felt its coldness and noticed how dark and silent the entire cottage was.

Though the room was dark, he instinctively navigated his way to the desk. He sat in the chair, struck a match and lit the oil lamp with it. He looked above the desk and gazed at his sword hanging on the wall. The flickering of the flame from the lamp caused dancing reflections on the sharp, clean shaft. He wondered if his past of war, death and killing were to be all that he would achieve with his life. His thoughts drifted to Violetta, and he convinced himself that his feelings for her would remain unrequited.

Being alone offered him a prime opportunity to release his

suppressed emotions. However, his stoic military attitude took over, and with it so went the chance. He collected himself and turned his attention to the pile of papers lying on the desk.

After several hours of working under the light from the lamp, his eyes grew too tired to continue any longer. He stood, picked up the lamp and went to his bedroom. He changed into his bedclothes and lay down on the bed. It was the first time he had done so since he brought Violetta to his home. He had permitted her to add some decorations and other little trinkets to the room to make it more comfortable for her during her stay. The room now had taken on some of her personality, much of it remaining as she had packed only her clothing before she left.

He had become accustomed to her presence, and her absence created an additional void that even his long-time companionship with Potter would no longer be able to fill. He laid his head on one of the pillows. As he began to fall asleep, he could smell the scent of the perfume that he had given her as a present. The fragrance was locked in the bedding fabric. He looked across the bed and imagined her lying there, looking upon and smiling at him. He reached out, but the other side of the bed was empty. In his drowsy state, he could not stop a couple of tears from falling. He then fell asleep.

XVIII.

Mid-October brought colder and much wetter weather. The number of suspects detained and questioned by the police dropped, but still no one was charged with the murders. The press continued its relentless coverage of the events and criticism of the police, which served to sustain the anxiety of the people and sell more newspapers.

Potter sent word to Johnstone that he was almost finished with helping the Morrison family and would be returning to the cottage in the next day or two. Johnstone had still not heard from Violetta, which caused him to be in a slight depression over her absence.

Despite the weather conditions, Johnstone ventured to the East End almost every night. He dressed in unkempt clothing to help himself blend in more with the local populace. His purpose for going there was two-fold, although he would not admit to himself which purpose had the higher priority. Certainly, he was there to do the job requested by Sir Charles. He believed he owed that to his fallen comrade and the victims. However, he also went into the district looking to see if Violetta was back on the streets.

A week prior, he had stood across the street from what had been Violetta's pitch. He observed that another woman had taken over that location. He had not seen Violetta anywhere in the area. Not seeing her there gave him some solace. As his feelings for her grew, thoughts of her being with other men were like tiny daggers stabbing into his heart. He knew that he had no right to interfere with her life, and he understood why she was doing that kind of work. However, that did not have any affect on how he felt, and how much he wanted to take her out of that situation and give her a life where she would not have to resort to such activities in order to survive.

On his most recent night in the district, he spotted Violetta approaching her pitch. The other woman also was there and assumed an alert posture upon seeing Violetta approach. Johnstone, who stood across the street, feared a disturbance similar to the one that he witnessed in the Ten Bells Pub. However, as the two women met, he was relieved to see that they appeared to be talking civilly to each other.

They both talked for a considerable length of time, even turning down apparent offers from passing men. The two finally finished, embraced each other and Violetta walked away, back in the direction from which she had come.

Johnstone followed her, but remained on the other side of the street. He made no attempt to make his presence known to her, and his ragged appearance was ample disguise. He felt certain she would not be able to recognize him. Still, as he followed her, he felt cheap, like the cheap men who bargained for these women's favors. He watched Violetta intently, and then stopped as he felt that his actions were making her appear cheap as well. To Johnstone, she was worth so much more, and deserving of much more than what life had thrown at her.

She had passed a dark alley familiar to Johnstone, but he neglected to recognize it as he turned away from the scene and let Violetta go. He failed to see the blue fog gathered in the alley as it coalesced, and the being that emerged from it. The being stepped onto the main street and walked towards the other woman. He met her and escorted her to the same alley behind the Ten Bells Pub where he had taken Violetta. However, Johnstone did not see any of this activity as he had returned to his carriage and begun his journey home.

Johnstone had mixed emotions as he entered his dark and silent cottage. He simply stood by the door and thought to himself. He remained saddened at the loneliness he felt over missing Violetta, but he had been comforted in seeing that she did not appear to be engaging in the activity that had gotten her into trouble. He had given Violetta's mother enough money to take care of the room rent for two months. In addition, he had provided some additional funds for food. Initially, Violetta was not expected to return to her home for about two months. He wondered what would happen, once those funds ran out. What would Violetta do? He thought about what he could do, but his funds were not limitless. Taking care of two households, no matter how much he wanted to help, was taxing his finances even just for two months. Even so, Violetta was a proud woman. Johnstone knew that at some point she would object to any further help.

His meditation was interrupted by the sound of shattering glass coming from his bedroom.

"Potter, is that you?" he called, startled from the sudden noise.

There was no answer.

"Hello?" he challenged. "Who's there?"

Receiving no response, Johnstone darted towards the bedroom.

He heard a rustling sound and then silence as he entered the room. No one was there, but the window was open. He went towards it, but heard a crackling sound when he moved forward. The sound was the result of broken glass under his feet. He stepped past it and looked out the window. The night was dark and overcast; nothing could be seen outside. He ran outside and looked around the cottage. He saw no one, but the conditions of the night would not preclude someone hiding in the area. He listened for any sound. There was none.

Content that whoever it was had fled the scene, he returned to his desk in the front room and retrieved the oil lamp. He turned the wick higher to brighten the flame and returned to the bedroom. He smelled perfume, the aroma of which reminded him of roses. The light from the lamp revealed the broken bottle on the floor. It was the remains of a heart-shaped perfume bottle that he had given Violetta.

A cold breeze carrying an equally cold drizzle blew into the bedroom from the open window. Johnstone sniffed an additional aroma in the air, but it was mixed with the fragrance from the spilled perfume, and prevented him from discerning its nature. He picked up the broken pieces, disposed of the fragments, and then closed the window.

Johnstone readied himself for bed, but the aroma from the perfume was too strong for him to sleep in the bedroom. He went to the front room to sleep on the couch. The smell of the perfume was prevalent there as well, but not as strong. He lay down and tried to sleep, but the perfume brought back thoughts and memories of Violetta. For Johnstone it was to be yet another restless, lonely night.

XIX.

The next morning was crisp and sunny. Johnstone awoke to the sound of chirping birds. It was much later than he normally rose from bed. If one did not know that October was almost completed, the scene could have been mistaken for an early spring day.

As Johnstone began his day, he mentally planned his activities. He had an appointment with Sir Charles scheduled for the late afternoon. He went to his bedroom to dress, and again noticed the aroma of the perfume. It was still strong. The weather being mild, he opened the small window to the room to permit some fresh air to come in and dilute the odor.

He went to the kitchen, and as he did so noticed that during the time that Potter had been away, the cottage had fallen into a disorganized state. Potter was expected to return in the next day or two, and Johnstone did not want him to see the cottage in such a condition, and then be burdened with cleaning it. The time spent cleaning permitted Johnstone the opportunity to clear unneeded paperwork and clutter from his desk. Several items belonging to Violetta remained in his bedroom. He organized the items and packed them in a suitcase. He placed the suitcase near the door in the front room with the intent to give it to Violetta after his meeting at Scotland Yard. To complete his chores, he filled each oil lamp in the cottage and lit them, keeping the flames at a low level.

Noticing that the time to depart for London was approaching, he changed into a suit. He called for his coachman to bring the carriage around, and he rode to his appointment with Sir Charles. The colonel forgot to take the suitcase.

Johnstone and Sir Charles discussed the progress made in the investigation since the double event that occurred on the last day of September, almost one month ago. Suspects were detained and questioned, but all of them had been ruled out as the killer. Johnstone reported that his observations in the East End showed that the level of concern of the people there had diminished greatly. Immediately after the double event, the streets at night had been devoid of all but a few prostitutes and men. Now he had found that the people had taken to the streets as before.

Sir Charles showed Johnstone several boxes of correspondence received by the Metropolitan Police, all purported to be from the killer. Most were obvious frauds, but two had caught the interest of the investigators on the case. On October first, the day after the double event, the Central News Agency received a post card, written in the same handwriting as the "Dear Boss" letter that taunted those involved in the investigation. Sir Charles showed it to Johnstone, who read it.

"I was not codding dear old Boss when I gave you the tip, you'll hear about Saucy Jacky's work tomorrow double event this time number one squealed a bit couldn't finish straight off. Ha not the time to get ears for police. Thanks for keeping last letter back till I got to work again.

Jack the Ripper"

Johnstone handed the card back to Sir Charles.

"And," Sir Charles said, "on October sixth, a local newspaper received a letter that we believe was intended to threaten witnesses into remaining silent."

Sir Charles handed the letter to Johnstone.

"You though your-self very clever I reckon when you informed the police. But you made a mistake if you though I dident see you. Now I know you know me and I see your little game, and I mean to finish you and send your ears to your wife if you show this to the police or help them if you do I will finish you. It no use your trying to get out of my way. Because I have you when you don't expect it and I keep my word as you soon see and rip you up. Yours truly Jack the Ripper.

PS You see I know your address"

Johnstone handed the letter back.

Sir Charles continued, "Finally, on October sixteenth, George Lusk, the president of the Whitechapel Vigilance Committee..." he looked up at Johnstone, "I believe you know him if I'm not mistaken."

"Yes, I do," Johnstone answered. "We have met with him and some of his committee members several times. We share information with each other."

"Very good. He's a good man and trying to help us out. We are inundated trying to find this killer. Most of the officers are tasked with keeping a watch for this murderer and nothing else. Because of that, I don't have enough officers to investigate the other criminal elements in the East End. Crime there is escalating at a very fast pace. At least Lusk and his committee are helping to keep things in order with the minor crimes." Sir Charles took a deep breath, and then returned to the original subject. "Anyway, as I was saying, Mr. Lusk received a package by the post. He opened it and saw that it contained a letter, and something else."

"What?" Johnstone exclaimed.

He handed another letter to Johnstone. "Read this one."

Johnstone's temper over the killer was rising and his anger grew further as he read the letter.

"*From hell.*

Mr Lusk,

Sor I send you half the Kidne I took from one woman and prasarved it for you tother piece I fried and ate it was very nise. I may send you the bloody knif that took it out only a whil longer

signed

Catch me when you can Mishter Lusk"

Johnstone had read the end of the letter aloud.

"We had a police doctor look at it, and he confirmed it was a human kidney that had been preserved in wine. The doctor concluded that it was similar to the kidney removed from Catherine Eddowes, the second victim from the night that we had the double murder."

Johnstone shook his head, handed the letter back to Sir Charles and stared at the wall.

"Colonel," Sir Charles resumed, after giving Johnstone a moment to collect his thoughts, "we have every reason to believe that this killer is going to murder again. We are also concerned that he is beginning to identify witnesses and threatening them. So far, he has kept to the prostitutes. That's bad enough of course, but if he starts going after others…" He paused and then continued, "I believe that, as he states in his letter to Mr. Lusk, he will create a living hell out of the East End, which will spread to London and who knows where else."

"My God, Sir Charles," Johnstone responded, "this man has to be stopped! He is an animal preying on the innocent in the jungle!"

"I agree."

"But you tell me that the Metropolitan Police, the London Police and Scotland Yard are not even close to solving these murders!"

"You're correct. We bring in people for questioning, even the suspect who owned that leather apron we found at one murder scene. We can find no one who any witness can identify, or who doesn't have a legitimate alibi." Sir Charles began to show frustration over the matter. "People in the East End tell us one story. We start investigating it. Then other people tell us something else and we end up going around in circles. Letters come in all the time; almost all of them are false. There are gangs that are taking money from the prostitutes. They force them to pay in return for 'protection', which of course they don't really provide. If the women don't pay, they beat them up. Some young men pretending to be the killer come up from behind to scare the prostitutes. Some even put knives up against the women's necks. We don't have enough room in the jails here to hold all this scum."

"This is all totally insane! I have seen much of what you related to me, but I didn't realize it was so widespread."

"It is," Sir Charles replied, "and it isn't very safe in the East End, not that it ever was, but conditions have degenerated tremendously over the past month. This is going on even in the daytime."

"Unbelievable."

"Yes, and I certainly do appreciate the help you have provided us. We have received some valuable information that we otherwise would not have obtained. Unfortunately, it hasn't led us to the killer yet."

Sir Charles stood and walked from behind his desk. He approached Johnstone, who stood, and the two shook hands. Johnstone nodded and smiled at the recognition of the efforts made by his team. He then left and returned to his carriage to go home. He instructed his driver to take the carriage through the heart of the East End.

The evening was settling in as he entered Whitechapel. He ordered the coachman to proceed slowly as he looked out onto the scene that was transitioning from the daytime to nighttime activities. The street gas lamps, of which there were few, were being lit. Shops and street markets were closing. The taverns and public houses were beginning to attract crowds, as many of the workers and sailors arrived to drink the day's work away.

The number of prostitutes in the area increased, as they attempted to gather some of the pennies before the men spent them all on drinks. For most, the pennies would be the means by which they would be able to find a place to sleep in a dosshouse for the night, even if it meant sitting in a corner of a room and being tied to a bench or chair with a rope so they would not fall to the floor.

As he observed what had become for him an all too familiar scene, he agreed with Sir Charles' assessment, and believed that it was just a matter of time before the killer would add another victim to his total. The revulsion that Johnstone felt on his first foray through the district had multiplied many times over during his subsequent visits there. This feeling was enhanced by his knowledge that Violetta lived there as well.

The road that led to Thurrock, and his cottage, eventually wound away from the city and neared the river. There, Johnstone looked out upon the low glow over the water that he knew would slowly turn into the blue fog, deliver its terror and defy capture.

Johnstone found his thoughts beginning to race as he processed all of the information that he had received and the sights, sounds and foul smells that he encountered. In his military career, he had lived in what he had thought were some of the worst locations in the British Empire. Now, he was trying to recall if he had been anywhere that compared to the misery and conditions that he observed in the East End. He began to get a headache, and could think no more. He sat back in his seat, closed his eyes and tried to clear his mind. The gentle rocking of the carriage put him to sleep for the remainder of the journey home.

XX.

The coachman pulled the carriage up to the front door of the cottage. He shook Johnstone gently to wake him up. It took a moment, and then Johnstone, half-awake and half-asleep, stepped out of the carriage. He stumbled slightly in the gravel driveway, but quickly regained his footing and walked up to the cottage. Johnstone stood outside the door and watched as the coachman put the carriage and horse away for the night. The coachman then mounted his own horse and rode toward his home in Thurrock. Johnstone sighed deeply and went inside.

Shutting the door and entering the front room, Johnstone observed the low glow of the oil lamps casting a dim light on what appeared to be a dark figure that moved from the front room to his bedroom.

"Potter, is that you?" Johnstone called out.

He followed the figure to the bedroom. As he entered the room, he was physically prepared to defend himself against whoever was in the cottage. Johnstone realized he had inadvertently left the window to the room open when he departed earlier in the day. He saw the last wisps of a blue fog drifting out of the window.

"What the hell?" he muttered as he turned and ran out of the cottage. He went to the side of the building where his bedroom was located. There, he looked up and saw the blue fog drifting upwards and over the thatch roof.

Johnstone pointed defiantly at the fog and yelled, "Goddamn it! What do you want now? Show yourself and let's be done with this!"

The fog continued its movement over the roof. Seeing this, Johnstone remembered that he had left the front door open, which was where it appeared that the fog was headed. He quickly returned to the front of the cottage. The fog was gone; the door stood open.

Johnstone quietly and with extreme caution approached the door. Before entering, he paused to listen for any sounds coming from within. All was silent. Entering the front room, he stopped just inside the doorway and looked intently about the dimly lit room for any sign of an intruder. All was still. Johnstone moved inward towards his desk. Behind him, unseen, the door slowly began to close. Then, a small creaking noise from a metal hinge alerted him to the activity behind his back.

Johnstone turned in time to see a dark figure emerge from behind the door. The dim light from the oil lamps provided sufficient illumination for Johnstone to see the light reflecting off what appeared to be a slim, metal shaft. He saw the figure thrust towards him with the shaft. Johnstone moved to evade the intruder and defend himself. He lunged toward the figure in an attempt to tackle it. However, he was not quick enough as the figure had the blade in position to stab the colonel's upper left arm.

Feeling the pain of what Johnstone now knew was a long blade, he instinctively pulled away from the attacker. The blade came out of his upper left arm as he spun around and then once more moved forward in an attempt to subdue the intruder. The blade slashed through the air, just missing his chest. Before the attacker could thrust again with the blade, Johnstone grabbed the figure and knocked it down to the floor. As it fell, it dropped the blade that hit the floor with a loud clanging.

Johnstone reached down to pick it up before the intruder could regain control of the weapon. As he put it in his hand, he realized that he was holding his own service sword that normally hung on the wall over his desk.

The figure was moving and trying to stand. Johnstone knocked it back down and told it not to move. He then ran over to the desk and turned up the lamp. With the brighter light, he looked over and identified his attacker.

"Potter!" he exclaimed.

Johnstone rushed over to Potter to help him sit up.

"What in God's name do you think you were doing, man?"

Potter, now in a sitting position on the floor, realized that he had attacked Johnstone.

"Dear Lord!" Potter was apologetic. "I thought you to be a burglar or something! I had no idea that was you. I am dreadfully sorry, Sir!"

"That's all right, Potter. Calm down, it's over." Johnstone was still holding the sword. "What the hell were you doing?"

Johnstone went over to the desk, put the sword on it and sat in his chair. Potter, groaning as he slowly rose, stood and went over to sit on the couch. Both men took deep sighs as their adrenalin levels returned to normal.

"I arrived home earlier tonight," Potter began. "You weren't here, so I prepared myself a little something to eat and retired to my room. I fell asleep, but was awakened when I heard shouting coming from outside. I rose from my bed and came out to the front room where I found the door standing open. Not knowing what was going on, I took the sword and hid behind the door. Then…"

"I know the rest, Potter."

"Yes, Sir."

Johnstone flexed his wounded arm.

"Did I…" Potter began.

"Yes, I'm afraid you did."

Potter went over to Johnstone. "Let me take a look at that."

Johnstone was still wearing his overcoat, which Potter helped him remove.

"Hmm, lucky for you that you were wearing your coat. Looks like the blade only caught the fleshy part of your arm. I'll clean and bandage it for you. Just stay here as I go get what I need."

Before he left, Potter picked up the sword and returned it to its proper place on the wall above the desk. One of the dowels used to hold the sword on the wall fell from its hole, causing the sword to fall onto the desk. Potter began to pick up the sword again.

"Potter, please leave things as they are, and get what you need to patch me up."

"Yes, Sir. Sorry. Right away."

He quickly returned, put the medical items on the desk, then went to his room and came back with an oil lamp. He put it on the desk and turned up the wick. The two lamps provided better illumination for Potter to tend to Johnstone's arm.

Johnstone spoke while his aide worked on the arm, "I believe that our friend was inside the cottage when I arrived home tonight. I chased a blue fog out of my bedroom window. I thought it was coming back inside because I left the door open. That is why I was cautious coming back in. When I saw the flash of the blade, I thought it was the killer we've been trying to find."

"Hmm, I noticed a heavy odor of perfume. It was Miss Karanova's wasn't it?"

"Yes, there was another night when I came home and I heard someone in my bedroom. When I went to the room, there was no one there, but the perfume bottle had been dropped and broken on the floor."

"I wonder if it's the perfume that is attracting him back here. He must think that Miss Karanova is still here and is following her scent."

"Potter, if that's true, then maybe we can set a trap and catch him here."

"Yes, that might be a possibility…"

"Ouch! Potter, that hurt!"

"Sorry. I'm cleaning the wound." Potter apologized and then resumed, "But anyway, there is one good thing about this."

"What's that?"

"If this being thinks that she is here, then he isn't looking for her in the East End. She should be safe for now."

"I hope so. I don't want her to have to go through that again."

Potter gave Johnstone a slight pat on the back, "All right. All finished. It should be completely healed in a few weeks, so take it easy with that arm!"

"Yes, Doctor Potter!" Johnstone joked.

Potter cleaned up, including repositioning the sword back on the wall above the desk. The loose dowel caused a slight problem, but Johnstone held the dowel while Potter placed the sword in its correct position on the wall. They then retired for the night, even though it would soon be morning.

Both men slept well into the morning. At breakfast, which was actually almost noon, Johnstone updated Potter on his activities in the East End over the past week.

The two stayed home for the next few days. They kept apprised of news regarding the investigation by reading about it in several different newspapers that Johnstone had subscribed to in addition to the *Times*. They were shocked to read a growing number of vicious articles and editorials attacking the obvious inability of the police to catch the killer. The attacks were growing in harshness, especially against those in charge of the investigation, including Sir Charles.

XXI.

In the late afternoon of October thirtieth, two women were talking over tea in a small first floor room of a run down tenement house at 13 Miller's Court in the East End. The walls were bare, with exposed concrete blocks revealing the building's construction. The door opened to a narrow passageway that was often used as a short cut to get back and forth to the pubs located on the streets on each end of the court. There were two soot-covered, multi-paned windows on the wall nearest the door. Improvised curtains for the windows consisted of sheets hanging from a rope. A small table stood by the farthest window. The back wall contained a fireplace and a cupboard, with a single bed and another small table beside it in the remaining corner. A couple of rickety chairs complimented each table. There was very little else in the room, and what was there was far from new.

"Julia, I don't see why you're getting all upset over this," Mary Jane said.

"It's not that I'm upset," she replied, "I don't think Joe likes your allowing me to share the room with you."

"Oh nonsense!" Mary Jane countered. "Joe knows why you're here. You lost your room and needed a place to stay for a little while."

"That doesn't mean he likes it. The room is small and we get in the way of each other."

"There are usually only three of us here, Love. Other rooms like this have over a dozen people staying in them. At least we try to pay the rent, even though I'm about two weeks behind at present. Anyway, it's much better in here and I want to keep it from looking like it does outside with all the people all over the place."

"Yes, it is nice to get away form all that noise and those people, and those disgusting men."

The sound of a group of boisterous men heard walking past the narrow passageway caused Mary Jane to change the subject.

"It's getting late!" Mary Jane said, as she put down her cracked teacup. "We'd better get out there before all those blokes drink up their pennies!"

Julia started to help clean up.

"No, no!" Mary Jane stopped her. "You go! I'll clean up."

Julia stood up from the bed, went over to Mary Jane and kissed her on the cheek. "You're a good friend," she smiled.

"You too," Mary Jane responded, as they hugged. "Now go on out among those disgusting men, and don't forget the signal!" she laughed.

Julia nodded her understanding, then walked to the door. "See you later," she said, as she left.

A few hours later, an intoxicated Joseph Barnett arrived home at 13 Miller's Court. He found a white handkerchief on the door handle.

"Oh, bloody hell," he slurred as he staggered into the room.

Julia was naked on the bed with an equally naked man with whom she was sexually engaged. Preoccupied in their activity, the couple did not notice Barnett's entry into the room. He stood over them swaying, "Get out, you damn son-of-a-bitch!" he yelled.

The man, startled, jumped off the bed. "Who the bloody hell are you, mate?" he challenged, although standing there naked in front of Barnett he appeared more comical than intimidating.

Julia sat up and extended her arms towards the man, "Love, it's all right!"

"No," the man responded loudly, "I want to know who the bloody hell he is!"

Trying to stand straight and look authoritative, if such were possible given his inebriated state, Barnett qualified his presence, "I am the man of this house, and I want you out of here now!"

The man looked back at Julia, "Lady, you didn't tell me you had a man!"

"I don't have a man!" she said.

"Then who is this?"

"The boyfriend of a friend of mine. He's leaving right now, so please, Love, come back to bed!"

The man began to gather his clothes and get dressed. "I don't think so," he replied. "I'm not one to perform with another man in the same room!"

The man reached down to pick up the money he had left on the table near the bed and put it in his pocket.

"No, please!" Julia begged.

"I don't pay, if we don't finish!"

Barnett grabbed hold of the man and pulled and pushed him out of the room. Still being in a state of mostly undress, passersby took notice and laughed at the scene. Barnett slammed the door shut.

By this time, Julia had managed to get herself dressed.

"I don't want you whoring in my bed!" he yelled. "If you're going to do anything here in my bed, it'll be with me!"

"Not on your drunk, filthy life!" Julia responded defiantly. "You know this is Mary Jane's place, and she lets me stay and work here when I need to!"

Barnett jabbed at his chest with one of his hands, "I'm the man here, and I don't want your bloody ass here anymore, so get the hell out before I drag you through the door like I did your friend!"

Julia was furious and defiantly straightened her clothing, put on her cloak and bonnet and then left, slamming the door behind her. Barnett dropped onto the bed. His pants were soiled and obviously wet. He soon fell asleep from the effects of the alcoholic drink.

A short time later, Mary Jane returned home. As she opened the door, she could smell the odor of soiled clothing and beer. She walked over to the bed and looked down at Barnett lying there and snoring loudly. Disgusted at the sight, she went over to the fireplace where she picked up the half-filled water pail. She carried it over to the bed and poured the water out on top of Barnett's face.

The impact of the cold water produced the desired effect as Barnett awoke coughing, choking and spitting water from his mouth. Startled awake, Barnett struggled to rise from the bed. Water that had spilled onto the floor created a slick spot that he set his feet on while trying to stand. He lost his footing and tripped over the table before stumbling to the floor. He rolled over onto his hands and knees and maintained that position while he groaned.

It was difficult for Mary Jane to determine if the groans were the result of the fall, the lingering effects of the drink or a combination of the two. Nevertheless, she had had enough of him.

"Get up, you pig!" she commanded.

He looked up at her as best he could, and slowly rose to his knees.

"How dare you treat my friend like that!" she screamed.

"Your whore friend," he mumbled.

Mary Jane kicked him on the leg, eliciting more groans from him. "She's my friend, and she's a person, and that's enough! What we do to make money is our business. Living here in this dump of a city, we don't have many other choices. You knew that when you moved in with me!"

Barnett looked up at her, shakily stood, and then replied, "I make money!"

"When you work!" she angrily replied.

He pointed to himself. "I work."

"Yeah, you work, you lazy bloke! A couple of days a week!"

"It's not easy for a guy to find work here either, you know!"

"You don't want me whoring, but we have to have enough money to eat and pay rent. When you worked at the fish market, I didn't need to stand out on a pitch dealing with whatever scum comes along. Now we can't even pay the rent, and I don't want to go back out into the street to sleep in the alleys," she said, as started to cry.

"I didn't want to smell like fish every day for the rest of my life!"

"So now you stink like gin and beer every day! That's better? You drink up almost every penny that you earn!"

Barnett belched, and Mary Jane noticed the now semi-dry spot on Barnett's pants become wet again and grow larger.

In disgust, she exclaimed, "Oh, this is just fine! Look at you! You're one drunken slob. I can't go on like this. I want you out of here!"

"What the hell are you talking about?"

"You, Joe! That's what I'm talking about! I can't go on living with you like this. Please, get your stuff and leave now!"

She walked over to the door and opened it. Barnett picked up the cup from the table and threw it at Mary Jane. He missed her and it broke one of the panes of glass on the window nearest the door.

"Fine!" he yelled. "Be a damn bitch. See if I care. I've had enough of you and your whore-friends hanging around here all the time anyway!"

"Get out!"

Mary Jane went to the bed and threw herself on it at the end closest to the corner of the room. She sat still, crying and staring at the barren wall. Barnett began gathering his belongings and put them in a sack. He did not own much, and what he did was mostly in a pile by the fireplace. He was far from quiet while he packed, as he slung drunken insults towards her.

When he finished, Barnett put the sack over his back. Mary Jane continued to ignore him and look at the wall.

He looked at the open door and then looked at her. He was much softer spoken as he said, "I'm sorry it didn't work out, Mary Jane."

She did not respond.

He again looked at the door and then at her. "Can I come around and visit you?" he asked.

"Only if you're sober," Mary Jane answered quietly, "but you can't stay here anymore. That won't work. It didn't work."

"All right, if that's what you want"

He went over to the cupboard and took out a small towel. He walked over to the window and put the towel into the opening of the broken pane of glass. He stood by the door and looked back at Mary Jane, "In a day or two?"

She nodded.

"You're a pretty lass, Mary Jane," he said as he left.

She resumed crying for a short while longer. When she ran out of tears, she picked up the pail and carried it outside to the water pump where she filled it with water. She returned it to its spot by the fireplace. She dipped a handkerchief into the pail and patted it on her face. She heard someone enter the room.

"Joe?" she called. Her back was to the door and she was unable to see who had come inside.

"Mary Jane?" was the surprised response.

She turned and was startled to see Julia, who was with a male partner. Julia's reaction was similar as she opened the door and double-checked the handle.

"Mary Jane, I didn't know you were here!"

"I'm sorry, Julia," she said. "Things got a little out of hand with Joe."

Julia's partner began to fidget.

"Oh, I'm sorry!" realized Mary Jane. "Let me just grab my wrap and bonnet, and I'll be on my way."

Julia asked the man to be patient a moment longer and she walked up to Mary Jane. "Are you sure?" Julia whispered. "I could go back in the alley with him. You know they don't care where we do it with them."

"You're sweet, but I'll be all right. You stay here. I'll leave."

"All right, then," Julia responded. She reached into her small handbag and gave Mary Jane a white handkerchief.

Mary Jane nodded, put on her wrap and bonnet and went outside. She tied the handkerchief around the outside door handle, and then walked through the court until she reached the street. There she walked past her usual pitch and entered The Britannia, a local public house. She looked about, seeing who was there. A woman, Maria Harvey, was sitting alone at a small table. Mary Jane walked over and joined her. The two had known each other for a short while, and Mary Jane had shared her room with Maria several times in the past.

The two sat together for a while, talking, sharing a small plate of food, and each drinking her own preferred beverage. The men in the pub knew the women as well, and several walked over to the table. The women brushed off their advances. Maria had been looking for Mary Jane to ask her if she could stay in her room for a couple of nights later in the week. Mary Jane was never one to decline a request from one of her fellow workers who needed a place to sleep.

Maria left after finishing a couple of pints. Mary Jane stayed behind for her third. As the night wore on, Mary Jane's intoxication grew. The males in the pub, like dogs after a bitch in heat, sensed her condition and stepped up their efforts to secure her services. She had begun signing her favorite Irish song, "A Violet from Mother's Grave." Even when intoxicated, her voice was still sweet, though much louder than normal.

She stood and started walking through the pub as she continued to sing. A drunken sailor grabbed her hips from behind and pulled her into his body.

She stopped singing, and loudly exclaimed, "What the bloody hell do you think you're doing?"

She tried to break away from his strong grip.

"Come now," he slobbered in his German accent, "let's leave and go at it."

She back-kicked him with her heel hitting his shin. The sailor yelled in pain and released his grip on her.

Mary Jane turned around, faced him and screamed, "I wouldn't even walk down the street with a pig like you!"

The sailor was furious. "No woman treats me like that!" he exclaimed. His fists were clenched as he started towards her.

A couple of his seafaring companions came up to him and tried to hold him back.

"Come now, Carl," one said, "no sense getting into a fight with a whore."

He broke free from their loose hold on him. Mary Jane suspected the sailor would retaliate. As he came towards her, she reached over to a nearby table, picked up a pint of ale and doused the sailor in his face with the drink. The alcohol in the beverage stung his eyes. He angrily screamed as he rubbed his eyes and called for a towel.

With the sailor distracted, Mary Jane ran out of the pub and stopped at the street corner, the act of which drew an instant objection and challenge from a prostitute standing there. Mary Jane cussed her response at the other woman, which incensed her even more. Before the situation could escalate any further, Mary Jane gave the other woman a slight push out of her way and quickly walked in the direction of The Ten Bells Public House, no too far distant.

Standing outside The Ten Bells, she debated with herself whether to enter or continue to another location. While deciding, she heard footsteps approaching from behind. Thinking it was the sailor, she assumed a defensive posture and turned around to face him. She relaxed as she saw a well-dressed man in a long cape and hat walking towards her.

"Good evening, my dear," he greeted her in his eastern European accent. He bowed slightly and tipped his hat to her.

She sniffed and smelled a lavender scent coming from him. It was pleasing to her, as was his appearance. Thinking she might be able to get him to pay a higher amount so she could take care of the rent, she smiled and returned his greeting, "Hello, Love…" Her voiced drifted away.

She had made eye contact with his controlling, red eyes, and she entered a trance-like state. He took her left hand and put it on his right arm. He then slowly escorted her around the corner from the pub and into the dark alley.

XXII.

"Come on! Come on! Are you all right, Miss?" a police constable called to Mary Jane as he also poked her in the side with his baton.

"Huh?" she responded groggily as she lay on the cobblestones in the alley.

The glare from the constable's bulls-eye lantern hurt her eyes as she tried to open them.

"I said, 'are you all right, Miss'?" he repeated. "If you can't stand up, I'll have to take you in for being drunk."

"No," Mary Jane objected, "I can get up." She started to move, "Please, Constable, if you would be so kind as to take my hand and help."

He did as she requested, and saw that she was able to stand on her own.

"You should go home now, Miss, straight away," he instructed. "The 'Ripper's' a-foot at night, and I would not like to find a lovely lass like you to have fallen to his knife."

She gave him a nervous smile and nodded, "Thank you, Sir. I will go home directly."

She started to walk, but staggered slightly. The constable grabbed hold of her arm to keep her from falling.

"If you've had too much of the drink to walk, Miss…"

"No, it's not that," Mary Jane interrupted, "I just feel weak."

"Here now, what's this?" he asked.

"I'll be all right. I just stumbled on a couple of cobblestones.

Just needed to find my footing."

"No," the constable said, "let me have a look."

"Look at what?"

"Your neck," he answered while moving his lantern closer to her.

"What do you see?" Mary Jane asked, as she was becoming anxious.

"Miss, I must ask you to come with me now."

"But, I was going home like you told me. I am not drunk," Mary Jane spoke, trying to avoid being arrested. "Just let me go home, please! I'll be all right now. I just stumbled, I told you. You can follow me home if you want, and see. It's not far."

"No, Miss, I have my instructions. I must take you to hospital."

"Hospital? What for?"

"You have two marks on the side of your neck. There's a bit of blood there as well."

"Marks?" She gingerly felt the side of her neck with her fingers. She looked at her fingertips and saw some crusted blood. "What does this mean?"

"That's for the doctor to say. For now, come with me out to the street. I will fetch a cab and take you to hospital."

"But..." she was extremely nervous.

"That's all I can say about it, Miss. I don't know anything other than those are my instructions if I see marks like that on someone's neck."

The constable hailed a cab, and instructed the driver to take them to Royal London Hospital. He assisted Mary Jane into the cab.

"I shall have to ask you some questions about your activities tonight, Miss," he stated as he got into the cab.

The driver snapped his whip and drove his carriage to the hospital.

XXIII.

In the early morning of the thirty-first day of October, an hour after dawn, the door to the slum room at 13 Miller's Court slowly opened.

"My God! My God!" Julia exclaimed as she jumped off the bed and ran to the door to embrace a physically exhausted Mary Jane as she entered the room. "Where have you been? I was pacing the floor all night. I was worried that he had gotten you!"

"Who?"

"Joe!"

"Oh, my poor Julia," Mary Jane tried to calm down her frantic friend.

They went over to the bed, where Mary Jane began to tell Julia what had happened. However, Julia saw that May Jane was too tired to continue, and told her to lie down on the bed to rest.

"But you wanted to know," Mary Jane said sleepily.

"You poor Dear! You rest now. You can tell me when you wake. I can wait."

"You're a good friend," she said as she fell asleep.

Julia remained in the room and kept still while Mary Jane slept. A couple of times she lay down on the far end of the bed and napped, she also being tired from staying awake all night waiting for Mary Jane to return home.

Later that afternoon, Julia was preparing to cook a meager meal for the two. She left the room with the pail to get some water from the pump located around the corner from the narrow passageway.

When she returned, she saw that the door to the room was open. She rushed inside and saw Barnett standing near the bed.

"What are you doing here?" She challenged him, though in a whisper so as not to awaken Mary Jane. "Trying to finish what you started last night?"

"What are you jabbering about?" He replied in a somewhat boisterous manner. "I see Mary Jane got real pissed last night, didn't she?"

"Shh," Julia insisted.

"What?"

"Shh," she repeated. "She's not drunk."

"Oh," Barnett responded in a much quieter voice, "stretched her legs too much then, eh?"

"No, you pig! It's not that. She was in hospital! What did you do to her?"

"Do to her? I did nothing to her! I hadn't even seen her since I left yesterday."

They were both whispering now.

"You haven't seen her?"

"No, I just came around to see how she was doing today. She said I could if I hadn't had anything to drink."

"I'm sorry, Joe. I'm just too upset. She came home this morning and said she was in hospital. I thought maybe you…"

"In hospital? What for?" he interrupted.

"I don't know. She fell asleep before she could tell me."

Barnett looked at Mary Jane as she slept on the bed. "She is such a lovely lass…" Then he got angry. "If some bloke did something to her..."

"I think it best if you leave now. Come back tomorrow. She'll be better then."

"All right," he said reluctantly. "You'll stay here with her?"

"Yes, she's my friend."

"All right." He looked at Julia. "Maybe I had you thought wrong."

"Too much drink will do that."

"Hmm, too much drink is about all one has to live for here," he replied, as he left.

Julia returned to her cooking. As the food warmed, the aroma woke Mary Jane. The two women sat on the bed and ate while Mary Jane told Julia about the previous night.

"Yes!" responded Julia, when Mary Jane had finished. "I have seen a blue fog. But green, grey or blue, it's all pea soup in this cesspool."

"And what about that gentleman?" Mary Jane asked. "He came to me last night looking just like the constable told me, but I don't remember anything after he walked up to me. The next thing I remembered was the constable waking me up."

"Hmm," Julia thought, "he does sound familiar, but I have never seen him." She thought some more and then snapped her fingers. "I have it!"

"What?"

"Remember one night in September? We were drinking a pint in Ten Bells. In comes these three gents with a lady that looked like they had taken their way with her. She was badly pissed, and couldn't stand. Remember?"

"Yes," remarked Mary Jane. "That was the Russian girl who was working a pitch near the pub."

"Yes, but Annie, bless her poor soul, almost got into a big row with her in the pub."

"I remember. One gave Annie some coins and she let them be."

"You were in the back with Annie, but I was sitting closer to them. I heard them talking strange things, but definitely about someone who sounded like your gentleman."

"Do you suppose he's the 'Ripper'?"

"I don't know, Love, but I do know that while the Russian girl survived with those men, Annie went out and was cut up in pieces."

"Then why didn't he do me in like Annie?" Mary Jane felt a cold chill run through her body.

Julia thought a moment, "The constable! He must have scared the sorry bastard off when he walked into the alley!"

"And Julia…the marks on my neck! He must have started…oh my God!"

Mary Jane hugged Julia and wept uncontrollably. Neither woman went outside that night.

XXIV.

The sun, just barely lighting the sky, found Johnstone and Potter finishing their breakfast. After several days of rising uncharacteristically late, they had resumed their normal waking regimen.

"Well, Potter, we made it to November. Just two months left in the year. Where did it go?"

"I don't know," Potter replied as he began to clear the table.

Johnstone rose from the table, "I think I'll get ready and ride into Thurrock this morning."

"Another letter?"

"What do you mean?"

"Nothing."

"Certainly you meant something by that comment. Come on, Potter, let's have it!"

"I was just concluding that you were going to Thurrock, and would probably visit the post office to send another letter to Miss Karanova."

Johnstone cleared his throat and a slight blush came upon his face, "You know that I've been writing to her?"

"Thomas," Potter started, with a rare break in protocol, "I have noticed for some time that you had acquired a fondness for the young lady."

"It was that obvious?"

"Well, how should I put it? When someone who hasn't been in love falls in love, there is an unmistakable glow about that person."

"A glow?"

"A glow of happiness. It is easily seen."

Johnstone sighed, "I wish I knew how she felt towards me, Potter. I feel incomplete and empty without her here. I wish she had told me one way or the other how she felt about me. At least I would know." Johnstone shook his head. "Do I seem to be acting like a school boy over this?"

"I do see that frustration in you, but no one knows what love will do or what direction it will take. I do know that she appreciates what you have done for her. You also spent much time together as she got better."

"And would that not have given her time to fall in love with me the way I fell in love with her?"

"You told her how you feel for her. That probably confused her."

"How so?"

"She had an abusive husband who died and left her with a child. She may not be ready to start a new relationship."

"But I wouldn't be anything like her husband was."

"Yes, that's true of course. However, there is a matter of her need to learn to trust again. She was, and continues to be, hurt. She asked you to give her time to think about it. Remember what she is and what you are. I'm sure that's playing into her confusion. Just let her be. She does have a little more time to go before she's back to herself again according to the doctor. If it's meant to be, you'll see her again."

"I suppose, Potter, but it's this not knowing…and not hearing from her…"

"I understand."

"Well, in any event, I'm going to town after I get dressed and will post my letter to her."

Johnstone prepared to leave and walked out the door. However, he came right back inside. He called for Potter, who came running into the front room.

"What is it?"

"Potter," Johnstone was holding several newspapers "look at this!"

"Not another…"

"No," Johnstone interrupted. "Look at the headlines!"

They read each one. Every newspaper was reporting about an attack by the "Ripper" that was thwarted by a police constable.

"Oh my God!" exclaimed Johnstone. "Potter, does the paper you're reading give a description of the suspect?"

"It certainly does, and it sounds just like our friend!"

"Yes, indeed it does! Finally, there's a witness who has seen him too!" Johnstone paused a moment, and then asked, "Potter, what day is it?"

"The second, Sir."

"No, I meant what day of the week is it?"

"It's Fri…" Potter started, and then became alert. "It's Friday, Sir!"

"We have to get back there! It's the weekend. Every murder has been committed on a weekend, and it's been over a month since the last!"

The men quickly saw to their tasks for the day, and then around mid-afternoon rode into London. With a few hours to spare, they made a courtesy call on the Morrison family. The widow reported that after Potter had finished helping her settle her late husband's affairs and returned home, she began to hear strange noises at night in the apartment. Periodically a blue fog would appear outside the building. She also stated that she was finding items in the apartment that had been moved and that others were missing, but she had never seen any evidence of someone breaking into the apartment. She also recollected smelling a flowery scent in the mornings when she woke, but was not sure what kind it was.

Johnstone asked her if he could look at her neck. She was confused over the request. He informed her that he wanted to make sure she was not experiencing the same trouble as Violetta had. Trusting her late husband's friends, she consented. She turned down the ruffled collar on her dress for Johnstone to see. He examined her neck, and was pleased to find that it was void of the marks that he had suspected might be there.

They stayed with the widow for a short while longer. She needed help with a few minor things. They assisted her and then left.

After visiting the Morrison family, Johnstone wanted to see Violetta. Potter strongly advised against it, calling to Johnstone's attention that the being appeared to be stalking the cottage, and now probably Morrison's home. Potter's premise was that the creature could be searching for Violetta's location. If they were to visit her now, they could be leading the being directly to her, especially since it was now dark. Reluctantly, Johnstone agreed.

They boarded the carriage with Johnstone entering first. Just as Potter began to climb onboard, he heard his name called.

"Potter, I am watching you," the voice softly spoke.

Potter stopped and stepped back down to the street. "What did you say?"

There was silence.

"Come out! Show yourself!" Potter demanded.

"Potter," a confused Johnstone called, "what on earth are you saying?" Johnstone poked his head out the carriage window. "Who are you talking to?"

Potter looked into the dark corners in the area, but saw nothing.

"Sorry, but I thought I heard someone call my name."

"I didn't hear anything. Climb aboard so we can get going."

Potter did as instructed, but as the carriage started to move, he looked intently out the window for any sign of someone hiding in the dark shadows. He saw nothing.

They rode to the East End and began their surveillance of the area. The Friday night crowds in the East End streets, taverns and public houses were large. The two men were surprised to hear little to no talk of the "Ripper", or of the report of the attempted attack from two nights prior. When the men tried to talk about it to those they met, the responses they received bordered on apathy. It had been over a month since the double event, and the people were of the opinion that life was returning to normal.

Despite the terror caused by the "Ripper" murders, the seventy-thousand people who lived in the one square mile known as the East End continued to have their share of murders, shootings, stabbings and assorted criminal acts, but these were considered "normal" for the district. A loud cry of "murder" was commonplace, and generally received little notice. The brutality and frequency of the "Ripper" murders, however, had stunned the populace. Nonetheless, as time had passed without a further act from the killer, the slayings were passing from the memories of the people.

Johnstone and Potter returned to the East End on the following night and remained there well into early Sunday morning. They ventured through as much of the Whitechapel and Spitalfields areas as possible. As with the preceding Friday night, the people they saw and talked to were more concerned with their drink and other affairs. For Johnstone and Potter, their surveillance had become an exercise in frustration. They heard nothing new, and they saw nothing on their own that would serve to help the police with the investigation.

With disappointing results for their efforts, each night they returned home exhausted. On each of those nights, upon their arrival home, it appeared to them as if some small, personal items had been moved about and were out of place. They could not be sure, but it was as if someone had been rummaging through their belongings, although the door and the windows to the cottage were still shut and locked when they entered the cottage.

"Potter, this is unnerving to return home and find that someone has been inside while we were away."

"Indeed. This is similar to what Mrs. Morrison told us. I suspect it is the being that we're looking for who is paying us visits. He must be looking for Miss Karanova."

"I hope he doesn't find her. We must think of a way to set a trap for him."

"It will be most difficult to do that. He is too powerful when he prowls around in the night."

"Then we must find him when he is at rest."

"That might be impossible."

"Why do you say that?"

"Because he seems to live in the fog. How can we capture that?"

"I don't know, but I would be beside myself if anything else happened to Violetta."

"I understand. We just have to think on this. The time eventually will be right. Then we will have our chance."

"Soon, I hope."

"We can only pray for that now, Sir."

On Monday, they were able to meet for a short time with Sir Charles. He informed them that changes were to be made in the investigation, as the Home Secretary had become involved. One of the minority political groups in the upcoming election was hoping to win the vote in the East End, and had begun sensationalizing living conditions there. They also were using the "Ripper" case to make their point that the government had abandoned the people in the district.

"Gentlemen, I'm at a loss of what to do anymore. I have more police officers in the area now than there ever have been. I have more investigators assigned to the case than have ever been used on a single case. Still, the attacks from the political groups and newspapers on our work continue."

"You're easy to target, Sir Charles," Johnstone said.

"Maybe, but the attacks aren't even logical!"

"How so?" Potter asked.

"I have brought my personal blood hounds to the murder scenes to try to track this killer. I am then criticized for wasting department resources. What resources? They're my dogs! Then when I don't use the dogs, I get criticized for not using the tools that I have available. What a dismal disaster this is turning out to be!"

"If you could just catch him," Johnstone said, frustrated, "life could go back to normal in Whitechapel, and everyone can move on."

"Oh, I'm sure the papers would still find something negative in how we captured him," Sir Charles complained. "Damn, I have asked several times for permission to post a reward for information leading to the killer's capture. They deny me even that! However, gentlemen, this is not your problem. It is now gone into the political realm, and of course, the politicians will do their best to botch things up with their brand of 'expertise'."

"No doubt," agreed Johnstone. "So, Sir Charles, do you see any further role for us in the investigation?"

Sir Charles shook his head and raised his hands in frustration. "You certainly have been a great help to us. I leave it to you. What would you like to do?"

"I think we'd like to continue with our work, as frustrating as it's been, at least until we are sure that the killer has been caught or the killings have stopped. What do you say, Potter?"

"I concur with you."

"All right then, gentlemen. I do appreciate your help and perseverance. The department continues to be indebted to you."

The two men continued their work in the East End over the next three nights. They came away each night with the same results as they had the previous week. The people preferred not to talk about the matter, they saw no blue fog, and there was no sighting of the being.

On Wednesday, before going to the East End, they made another visit to the Morrison family. The widow reported occurrences similar to those she described to them before. When they left the family and were boarding the carriage, someone spoke.

"Potter, I am watching you," the soft-spoken voice was heard again. "You shall not get away with this!"

"All right, that's enough!" Potter shouted.

"Potter?" called Johnstone.

"Sir, there is someone calling me," he responded, and then turned his attention back to the shadows. "Come out and face me! Let's be done with this!"

His challenge and demand went unanswered.

Johnstone stepped down from the carriage.

"Did you hear the voice?" Potter asked. "It was the same as last time."

"I heard nothing. Where do you think it came from?"

"I'm not sure. It was spoken so softly and my back was turned away from the area, but it had to have come from a dark area around here."

"Very well, let's take a look."

"In the dark?"

"Hmm." Johnstone spotted a constable walking towards them on the other side of the street.

Johnstone called to the constable and asked if he would help them search the dark recesses in the area around the Morrison's apartment building. The constable obliged them and used his bulls-eye lantern to illuminate several different areas. To Potter's chagrin, there was no one hiding in any location. They thanked the constable for his help, and then went on to the East End.

They stopped at The Britannia Public House. It was not too crowded, and they were able to secure a table for themselves about in the middle of the pub. They each ordered a bowl of stew and a pint of ale.

It was not long before Mary Jane walked in. She stopped near the doorway and surveyed the pub for potential customers whom she might be able to convince to go with her. She gave a frown at the available selection and walked towards the bar. She stopped when she reached Johnstone and Potter.

"I see you gents in many of the pubs all the time," she started, "but you don't drink much and I have never seen you leave with a lady."

Both men stood in a respectful greeting to the woman. She had been drinking, but not enough to make her intoxicated. They invited her to sit with them, which she gladly accepted. They introduced themselves just as the food and drink was brought to the table.

Johnstone noticed her looking at the bowl of stew. "Would you care for some, Miss Kelly?"

"I wouldn't want to put you out just for me."

"It's no bother at all." Johnstone called the barmaid and ordered a bowl of stew for Mary Jane.

"Could you possibly add a pint of beer to that order, Love?"

Johnstone nodded to the barmaid, who then left to fill the order.

"You know, we actually have met you before."

"No, I would remember talking to you two gentlemen, even if you are dressed in ratty clothes."

"You can see that we're not from here?" Potter asked.

"Oh, to be sure. Gentlemen have trouble hiding their ways. If you were from here, you'd never ask me to sit with you or even offer me food. No, you'd just pull out a couple of pence from your pocket and want to have a turn with me. That's all."

"See, Potter, and we were wondering why it was difficult to get people to talk to us. However, Miss Kelly, we have met before over in The Ten Bells Pub several weeks ago."

She looked at their faces for a moment, and then nodded. "Oh yes, I see now. I remember people's eyes. It tells so much about them. But, weren't there three of you? And you were with that Russian girl. You were sitting right over there," she pointed.

"Yes, that's amazing!" Potter exclaimed. "Annie caused a row that night," Potter reminded her.

"Yes." Mary Jane became serious. "God rest her poor soul. And Lizzie too. She was with us. Poor girls."

"Yes," Johnstone continued, "it was most unfortunate what happened to your friends."

The barmaid brought the bowl of stew and pint of beer for Mary Jane, place it on the table and left. Mary Jane took a pull from the mug and began to eat.

"No, we were not really friends," she remarked, while eating. "We were sisters, because of the work."

"Ah," acknowledged Johnstone. "I understand."

She stopped eating and became serious again. "Do you know what they say about Annie and Lizzie?"

"What do you mean?" Potter asked.

"Well, they say they were treated pretty badly. Like they were cut open like fish."

Johnstone took a deep breath, "That is one way to put it."

"How horrible to go that way."

"Yes, it was," Potter remarked. "Miss Kelly, have you heard anything or seen something that might give a clue as to who did this?"

"I don't know. There was much talk then, but I never saw anything, and the talk is gone now."

"Pity that," Johnstone observed.

"Have you seen a blue fog?" asked Potter.

"Fog?" she chuckled. "There's almost always something like

that around here."

"Well, Miss Kelly," Johnstone began, "you say you've seen us around the East End. If you ever find out anything that might help find this killer, please let us know."

"All right. Are you police?"

"No, but we are trying to help them."

"All right.

The men stood to leave.

"You haven't finished your stew," Mary Jane observed. "May I?"

Johnstone looked at her and nodded his head. She pulled the bowl towards her.

"Thank you."

Johnstone place a half-crown coin on the table near her.

"What's this?" she asked, surprised.

"For your time, Miss Kelly. We appreciate it. When you finish eating, please go home and stay there."

"I have to work. I have to pay the rent."

"Stay inside and be safe," Johnstone repeated, as the two men left the pub.

When they returned home, they once more saw that items had been moved about. In the front room, Johnstone was angered when he saw that his regiment banner had been slashed, presumably with his sword that was found lying on the couch. They checked the rest of the cottage. Nothing else had been damaged. The door and windows had all been shut and locked, and there was no sign of entry into the cottage.

"We have to find who is doing this!" Johnstone declared.

The next morning, the eighth day of November, they received a request from Sir Charles to meet with him in London as soon as they could. Potter offered to remain at the cottage to conduct his own surveillance to see who was entering their home while they were away. Johnstone agreed to the plan, and made haste to see Sir Charles. So that Potter would have transportation if he needed it, he drove Johnstone to Thurrock, keeping the carriage, while the colonel hired a cab to take him to London.

XXV.

November 8
** 12:15 P.M. **

Johnston arrived at Sir Charles' office shortly after noon, and found the Police Commissioner in a grim and somber mood. He was updated on the latest events pertaining to the investigation and changes that had occurred since they last met. It was not long before Johnstone had the same disposition as Sir Charles.

"…and so," Sir Charles concluded, "after a visit with the Home Secretary this morning, I tendered my resignation."

Johnstone sat stunned. "Could there have been any way to avoid this decision?"

"Colonel, we are both military men. Our abilities and the tactics that we used in the Queen's Service are different from what is required in police work. In the Police Commissioner's office, there is too much politics to muddle through. If I had not offered my resignation, I would have been forced out eventually anyway."

"Sir Charles. I am certainly sorry to hear that it came to this."

"Pay it no mind, Colonel. I knew it was coming, which is the real reason why I asked you here today. I should be cleared out of this office by tonight, but I wanted to share one last item with you while I am still able to do so."

Sir Charles picked up an envelope off his desk and handed it to Johnstone.

"More correspondence?"

"The letter was found yesterday in a pillar box. It was addressed to the police, and brought to my attention."

Johnstone opened the envelope, removed the letter and read it.

"Dear Boss. I shall be busy to-morrow night in Marylebone. I have two booked for blood – Your Jack the Ripper – Look out about ten o'clock, Marylebone road."

Johnstone handed the letter back to Sir Charles. "You think this to be genuine?"

"We receive so much correspondence from pranksters. Could it be real? It's possible. We don't have enough men to investigate every piece of paper that comes through with 'Jack the Ripper' written on it. The timing is right, however. I suggest you take a couple of constables with you and check it out tonight. It would be best if they aren't in uniform, but blast them, make sure they aren't wearing their police boots! Damn dead giveaway! We've been criticized for that too. Damn!" He pounded his fist on the desk.

"All right, I'll go there. No harm checking this out."

"Keep alert. Remember I am off the case, so work directly with the investigators if you come up with any new information."

The meeting ended shortly thereafter. The two men shook hands and parted company for the last time. Johnstone was not happy to have learned of Sir Charles' resignation. He believed that the act would prolong the investigation even more. However, Johnstone was not naïve, and understood that the political mood demanded quicker results.

** 2:30 P.M. **

After he left Scotland Yard, Johnstone paid a visit to the Morrison family. They were busy packing their belongings and preparing to move to Bristol where the widow's family lived. Potter had made arrangements for the sale of the larger items that they would not need to take with them. Johnstone made his farewells to the family and vowed to stay in touch with them.

Having completed his business with Sir Charles and the Morrison family, Johnstone had several hours to spare before nightfall. Without Potter to dissuade him, Johnstone decided to take the risk and visit Violetta. She had become a constant in his daily thoughts. With every beat of his heart, he felt her presence within him.

Before he left London, he stopped at a jeweler and purchased a necklace with a heart pendant. He intended to give it to Violetta. As he rode in the carriage to her lodging home, he removed the necklace from its case, kissed the heart and repackaged it.

At the lodging home, Violetta's mother answered the door. Her daughter had explained to her what had happened and what was stalking her. Johnstone was not permitted into the home, as Violetta's mother was fearful that he might have brought the evil with him. She held the door open only to the point that she was able to see out with one eye. She told Johnstone that Violetta was not there and had been out for most of the day. She did not know when her daughter would be returning home.

"I see," Johnstone said. "Could you please tell her that I

stopped by to see her?"

"No, Sir," Mrs. Karanova answered in English. "I not tell her. I no want her out tonight. Too much evil in city. I scare for my daughter. If something happen, Katrina have no mother."

"All right. I understand. I'm sorry for coming here and upsetting you. I just wanted to see Violetta. Thank you, Mrs. Karanova."

Disappointed at not finding Violetta at home, Johnstone left and went to The Britannia Public House, where he ordered a meal. He would remain there until it was time to go to Marylebone. While he waited, his thoughts continued to drift to Violetta.

** 4:00 P.M. **

Potter was busy with his household chores when he heard a carriage arrive. Assuming it was Johnstone, he continued with his work. A knock came at the door.

"He knows I'm here," Potter mumbled to himself, "and the door is not locked."

There was another knock at the door.

"Hmm, I wonder if he thinks it's locked and he forgot his key."

Potter went to the door and opened it just as the third round of knocks began. He was surprised at whom he saw.

"I sorry, Mr. Potter, to bother you."

"Not at all. Please come in, Miss Karanova."

She remained outside, and avoided looking at Potter as she was embarrassed at the request she was about to make. "Umm, I need take care of coachman. I no want to sound like beggar, but I have not any money."

"Oh! Yes, of course. One moment, please. Please tell the coachman I will be right there."

"All right."

Violetta did as instructed while Potter retrieved his purse. She stayed by the door and waited for him to return.

"Please, Miss Karanova, go inside and make yourself comfortable. I'll be back directly."

She nodded, went inside and sat on the couch. Potter went to the taxi and gave the coachman the amount needed for the fare.

The coachman took the money, put it in his coat pocket, winked and said, "You have a good time there, Governor! Shall I wait until you've finished so that I can take the lady back?"

Potter was insulted. "It is not like that at all!"

"It makes no matter to me, Governor. If you need me, I will be happy to oblige and wait for you, Sir." He winked again.

"That will be all! Your services will not be needed or desired. You may leave presently and return to London!"

"Very good, Governor. Thank you for the fare."

Potter returned to the cottage as the taxi left. He was infuriated by the encounter.

"What is it, Mr. Potter?" Violetta asked sensing his agitation. "You mad at me?"

"Oh certainly not, Miss Karanova!"

"It my fault. I should not have come here. Sorry for what I do."

"It is not your fault, and you have no reason to be sorry for anything. It's just that some people draw conclusions without having any facts, and assume things that are not true."

"I understand. Woman like me here is…inappropriate."

"You must not think like that! I certainly don't think like that about you, and the Colonel doesn't see you like that at all, either!"

"I understand, but still look bad. Where is Colonel?"

"He was called into London on business."

"Oh. Do you know when Colonel come back?

"Actually, I thought that was him when I heard the carriage drive up. However, it could be soon, or very late in the night before he returns home. I really do not know."

"Oh."

"Is there something I can help you with? Anything you need?"

"I came for rest of my things and talk for minute with Colonel."

"Well, I know that he packed your things. They are in a case in his bedroom."

"He packed my things?" She asked, sounding disappointed as she looked towards the bedroom.

"My word, I have just noticed the time is getting on. Would you like some tea and scones?"

Her eyes lit up and she exhibited her infectious smile, but she said, "I must get home now. I take enough of your time. I just get my case and take taxi back."

"I sent the taxi away. If you must leave now, I can take you home. However, it would be very nice if you would stay a while and have some tea with me. Maybe the Colonel will be back shortly. Then you can see him, and will not have wasted the trip out here."

Violetta sighed. "All right. I guess I stay little longer and see."

"It's all right. The tea will do you good, and I will enjoy your company again!"

"Very well," she smiled, "I have some tea. Thank you."

The two talked together for a long while. They spoke of the time that Violetta spent in the cottage while she was convalescing. She continually remarked about her gratitude for the help and kindness that Johnstone and Potter extended to her. She told Potter that while she was staying with them, she had felt safe, peaceful and wanted. Potter told her how much he enjoyed her company, and how much Johnstone cared for her. Violetta avoided commenting on what Potter said about Johnstone. She was very inquisitive, however, about the status of Colonel Morrison's family. Potter finally noticed how late it had become.

"I have totally lost track of the time again!"

"And fire in fireplace has gone down too."

"I will tend to it immediately. We do not want a chill now, do we?"

Potter tended to the fire while Violetta stood and looked out the window that faced the river.

"Looks like it going to rain. Clouds growing and fog over river," she reported.

"Oh yes," Potter replied as he stoked the fire, "it has been looking like rain almost all day." He put the fireplace tool down and wiped his hands on a towel located there. "Would you care for any supper?"

"I not want to be trouble."

"You are not any trouble at all."

She considered the offer. "You let me help cook?"

"That would be splendid!"

** 6:30 P.M. **

At 13 Miller's Court, Mary Jane was sharing a meager meal with Lizzie Albrook, a neighbor friend. They were sitting on the bed and using the nearby table.

She was in a reflective mood as she told Lizzie, "Whatever you do, don't you do wrong and turn out as I did. I am heartily sick of my life. I wish I had money enough to go back to Ireland to be with family. I would not do what I do, except I have to keep myself from starvation."

"Oh, Mary Jane, I know it hasn't been easy, but something good will come out of this for you. You just have to pray and trust in the Lord!"

Mary Jane pursed her lips and nodded.

"Well, I had better get home before he begins to miss me! He probably stopped at a pub on the way home from the docks and is drunk now!" she laughed.

"All right, Lizzie," Mary Jane smiled. "Thanks for coming and spending some time with me. It was nice seeing you tonight."

They stood up from the bed and gave each other a hug.

"Something good will happen for you, Mary Jane. Wait, you'll see."

Mary Jane smiled. Lizzie then turned to go to the door and opened it.

"Oh!" she exclaimed startled to see someone outside.

Mary Jane came up behind Lizzie. "It's all right," she said.

Lizzie left and Barnett walked in.

"Was I interrupting anything, Mary Jane?"

"No, Joe. Lizzie and I had a bite to eat and we were talking. She was just leaving."

Barnett nodded.

They both sat on the bed, but on opposite ends. The bed was more comfortable than the chairs.

"Mary Jane, you look very nice tonight."

"Thank you, Joe." She gave a little giggle, and was slightly embarrassed by the compliment.

"What?" he asked.

"Oh nothing."

"Come on. Tell me."

She hesitated, then said, "I was just thinking how nice it has been with you coming here every evening and spending time with me. We've had nice talks, and I miss you when you're not here."

Barnett smiled, "It has been good. Too bad we…"

"I know, but it's what it is, Joe."

"I think I'll be getting regular work again soon, Mary Jane. Do you think…"

"Joe," she interrupted again, "I don't know right now. We can talk about it later when we see how things go between us again. Is that all right?"

"If that's what you want."

"For now, yes."

"All right." Barnett took a deep breath, "Mary Jane, thank you for letting me come over and talk to you, especially after what happened. I'm sorry for that. It does mean a lot to me to see you."

"Me too, Joe."

"I'll stop by and see you again tomorrow night, all right?"

"I look forward to our little chats. They're nice. You don't have to run off so soon every time either. You can stay a little longer if you want."

"I don't want to be a bother to you."

"It's no trouble, Joe. I have time for you."

Barnett stood and walked over to Mary Jane. He took her by the hands and kissed them. She then stood and walked him to the door and saw him out.

** 8:00 P.M. **

Violetta and Potter had completed their supper and cleaned the kitchen. Afterwards, they sat at the table and talked. Violetta wanted to learn more of what had been happening in the East End. Potter told her what new information he knew. He did not tell her, however, the more sordid details about the slayings. Violetta also began to ask questions about Johnstone, particularly about how he was and if he had shared his feelings for her with Potter. He answered as best as he could.

As they talked, they once more lost track of time. The fire in the fireplace had burned down to just glowing embers. The small kitchen was able to maintain its warmth from the stove that still radiated some heat from the meal preparation.

The weather continued to deteriorate as the rain front moved inland. The fog became thicker and encircled the cottage. A bluish light within it began to glow as the fog drifted towards the chimney.

The two continued to drink tea and snack on biscuits as they talked and awaited Johnstone's return.

Violetta suddenly changed the subject of their conversation. "Mr. Potter, do you smell something?"

"What do you mean?"

"I smell flowers."

Violetta stood from the table and went to the front room. She called to Potter, "The fire out and smoke come into room!"

Potter rushed into the room. "What did you say?"

She pointed to the fireplace.

"Damn! We've been talking…Wait a minute!"

"What?"

"That isn't smoke, it's fog!"

As more of the fog entered the front room, its blue hue increased and its shimmering became brighter. Then as the two watched, it coalesced and a being formed by the fireplace. Its fiery red eyes glared in the dimly lit room. It stepped towards them. The light from the lamp on the desk illuminated its face.

"It man from river!" Violetta screamed.

"Oh my God!" was all that Potter could say.

** 8:30 P.M. (1) **

After Barnett left her room, Mary Jane freshened her appearance and stepped outside. She walked towards The Ten Bells Public House. While enroute, she met a friend, Elizabeth Foster. They talked for a moment before deciding to go together to the pub for some drinks.

The pub was not yet overly crowded and the women found an empty table near the front door. Mary Jane preferred to sit where she could face the door and watch the people as they came inside. A barmaid, who took their drink order, greeted the two women.

Barnett was sitting with some male friends towards the back of the pub. He noticed Mary Jane's arrival, but made no attempt to reveal his presence to her.

The women had one drink, then a second and then a third. Some of the male patrons in the pub made advances towards them, but were turned away, at least for the moment while the women still maintained a level of sobriety. However, that would soon pass.

Barnett, who had a couple of drinks more than Mary Jane watched the activity. His disdain over what he saw grew. He knew that Mary Jane had to work, and there was no other work available for her to do. However, he still had a small amount of jealousy, which gave him difficulty with the thought of other men engaging sexually with her. Finally, his tolerance level had been reached. He quickly finished his pint of ale and slammed the empty mug on the table. His companions were startled by the sudden noise. The pub fell silent for a few seconds as the other patrons tried to figure out what caused the sudden disruption, and what event, typically a fight, would follow next. The pub owner questioned Barnett regarding his behavior, but Barnett refused to answer. He stood and walked towards Mary Jane's table. He was unmistakably intoxicated as he stood over the women.

"Whores!" he yelled at them. Then he glared at Mary Jane, "You kicked me out of your bed, but you'd take anyone else who would give you two pence!"

He reached into his pocket, took out two pence and threw it at her. He then stormed out of the pub.

Mary Jane was furious over his behavior, and started to rise from the table to follow him.

"It'll come to no good if you chase after him, Love," Foster said as she took hold of Mary Jane's arm. "Sit, and be still," she instructed.

"That pig! How could he do that?"

"He's drunk, and you know how he gets when he's like that."

Mary Jane sat and started to cry. "He had been coming over and seeing me in the evenings. We have had such nice talks. He wants to come back to live with me. I was beginning to think he had changed, and was considering letting him come back. Now, tonight he has to go and do something like this! I can't let him come back and go through this again and again. I can't!"

"Finish your drink, Love. You'll feel better after that. If not, I'll buy you another."

** 8:30 P.M. (2) **

The time had come that it was necessary for Johnstone to leave the pub and start towards Marylebone Street in response to the latest threat received from the "Ripper". Following Sir Charles' instructions, he found two plain-clothes police officers with whom he had previously worked. Johnstone looked at their attire. They were not wearing their police boots.

They discussed the situation and devised a strategy whereby the three would move towards the area stated in the letter, but from three different directions. Each would approach from the south, walking up three side streets that were spaced several blocks apart. One officer would be on each end, with Johnstone in the middle. They would move from Whitechapel until they reached Marylebone Street. Johnstone would arrive in the heart of the area where most of the prostitutes worked. The two officers would converge on his location, one from each end of the street. They would watch all alleys and side streets as they made their individual approaches and be alert for anything suspicious.

They set out on their surveillance patrol, walking at a quick pace. The weather was becoming decidedly worse as they began, but the rain had not yet started.

As Johnstone neared his position, he slowed his pace to enable him to better observe the people in the area. The overcast sky hid a small, crescent moon. The gas lamps on the streets were spaced far apart, and the alleyways were mostly void of the lamps. Without the aide of artificial light, observations in the nearly black night were much more difficult.

Johnstone stopped when he reached a narrow alley one block from Marylebone Street. He peered down the alley and saw some movement. He walked into the alley as quietly as possible, keeping close to the buildings to avoid detection while he tried to discern who was there.

The light from a window briefly illuminated two people walking past it and in the opposite direction from where Johnstone stood. One was a woman who seemed to be staggering as she walked as if she were heavily intoxicated. The other, from the silhouette in the light, appeared to be a man wearing a long coat and top hat. A gentle, but damp breeze blew down the alley towards Johnstone. He detected a familiar floral scent.

"You there!" Johnstone called into the alley.

The couple continued walking, and tried to move faster. However, the woman's difficulty staying upright, and the need for the man to hold her up and pull her along with him, kept them from running away. Johnstone quickly followed them, and was able to decrease his distance from the couple.

"You there! I need to talk to you a moment."

They continued to ignore his hail.

"I'll call for a police officer if you don't hold where you are!"

With that threat, the two stopped. Johnstone slowed to a normal pace, as he was not that far away from them. Their backs remained turned towards him.

"I am sorry for the intrusion. This should only take a moment," Johnstone said as he neared. "I just need to ask you some questions."

When Johnstone had closed within a few yards of the couple, the man released his hold on the woman. She collapsed onto the alley, lying motionless and face down in the dirt. The man then turned and faced Johnstone. The bite of his searing red eyes was instantaneous. Johnstone was not anticipating this, lost his footing on the uneven cobblestones, and fell.

The being leapt into the air and pounced on him like a wolf attacking its prey. Johnstone did not have a chance to try to stand. The being picked up Johnstone by his shoulders, and held him at eye level. Johnstone felt the being's physical strength. He knew that any sort of struggle on his part would be difficult at best. He could tell that the being was attempting to gain control. Johnstone did what he could to try to keep from looking into its red-eyed stare. This angered the being, who tossed Johnstone like a sack of clothing against the nearest building. Johnstone's back hit against the bricks and he collapsed onto the narrow sidewalk. Some rotted mortar from between the bricks came loose and fell onto him. The being went over to Johnstone and again picked him up.

"I warned you and your comrades not to interfere with me," the being growled lowly.

"You cannot continue like this. You must be stopped!"

The being pushed Johnstone back into the wall, eliciting a painful groan from him, and, moving his face closer to Johnstone's, said, "You have no control over me. Neither you nor your remaining comrade can prevent me from doing what I must. The order in the world between the living and the dead must be maintained."

Johnstone could see the being's sharp fangs.

"You are not part of the order here. You can kill me now, but others will hunt you down and stop you and your killing!"

"It is not what you think!"

"No? It is you who foretold the police what you were going to do here tonight by turning your brutal killings into a game with your letters."

"Fool! What need would I have to write letters? You are misguided and interfering with what I must do!"

"You keep saying that, but women keep dying savagely by your hand. So what is it?"

The being had grown impatient and tired of the discussion. It leered at Johnstone. "Look into my eyes!" it commanded.

Johnstone continued his efforts to avoid eye contact.

"Damn you! You will look into my eyes or I will strike you down here and now!"

Johnstone finally lost the battle and fell under the being's control. It moved closer to Johnstone's face to the point that their noses were almost touching. Beads of saliva dripped from the being's fangs. Its hot breath, appearing like a fog in itself as it met the chilly air, circled Johnstone's face.

Johnstone winced as he felt a pain in the back of his head. The pain grew stronger as the being's eyes looked into his. Images began to appear in his mind. There were dark visions of many people. It was difficult for him to see clearly, as everything was out of focus at first. Then the visions became brighter and clearer and he saw images of women being murdered and then the murdered women lying on the ground. One by one, the images passed and then changed to just the faces of the women, which flashed separately in a constant rotation. Johnstone finally recognized them as the Ripper's victims.

Then he saw a face that he could not recognize. It had peering red eyes, but its features were distorted. He saw a vision of a funeral where he was holding one corner of the casket. Other pallbearers held the remainder of the casket. They wore black robes, and their faces were featureless, blank. The vision took on a physical nature, and it was as if he were actually carrying the casket. It weighed more than he anticipated and its weight pulled on his arm and hand to the point that he thought he would drop it. The funeral procession approached an open gravesite, and he held the casket over the deep hole. The bottom then fell out of the casket, and he watched as dirt that was hidden inside it, emptied into the gravesite. After all the dirt had fallen into the hole, the pallbearers released their hold on the casket. Johnstone could not carry the weight of the casket by himself, and he also let go of it. The casket fell into the hole. At the head of the gravesite, he now saw a gravemarker, and recognized the name. The vision then ended as Johnstone lapsed into unconsciousness. The being dropped him in the alley alongside the woman. It walked further into the alley, then transformed itself into a bat and flew away towards the river.

By this time, the woman was regaining her faculties. She began to rise and then saw Johnstone lying next to her. He lay on his back with his arms obscuring his face. She quickly looked around at her surroundings. She was uncertain as to where she was, and seeing an unknown man so close to her unnerved her. She began to scream loudly.

It did not take long for a police whistle to sound in response. A second whistle quickly followed it. A constable ran into the alley. His lantern illuminated the scene as a second constable arrived.

"It's him!" the woman screamed. "It's Jack the Ripper!" she continued to scream, as she pointed at Johnstone.

"What did you say, Miss?" asked the first constable.

"It's Jack the Ripper! He brought me here to do me in, no doubt! He knocked me out. I must have hit him in the head when I fell down. It's the Ripper!"

"John, you'd better call for more help, just in case she's right," the first constable instructed his partner.

"Bloody hell yes, Michael, if that's him!" the constable reacted, and then blew his whistle several times. "Michael, do you think she's right?"

The woman was now standing and began to distance herself from the scene.

"Best stay here, Miss," John instructed. "The investigators will want to question you about this."

"John, do you think we should move his arms and get a look at his face?"

The two constables bent down. Michael was holding his lantern close so they could get a better look. Two plain-clothes police officers had turned the corner and were running to the scene.

"Be careful, John. He may be faking it."

The woman backed farther away at the words of warning from the constable. John moved Johnstone's arm and revealed his face.

"That's him!" the woman exclaimed, as the lantern illuminated his face.

"Are you sure, Miss?" Michael asked.

"As sure as ever I was…I've seen his face before. He's been all over talking to the girls. He's The Ripper for sure!"

Johnstone began to stir. John grabbed his wooden truncheon from a belt loop and prepared to use it on Johnstone as the two officers arrived.

"What do you have here?" one of the officers said.

"This lady says this man is Jack the Ripper. Took her to this alley and was, well you know…" John reported.

"What? Let's have a look!"

"Blast!" said the other officer as they saw Johnstone's face.

"What's wrong?" asked Michael.

"He's not The Ripper."

"It bloody is him!" objected the woman.

"Then who is this?" asked John.

"This is Colonel Johnstone. We're working with him to hunt for The Ripper. We were supposed to meet him around the corner. He never showed."

"He's not The Ripper?" the woman asked.

"No, Miss."

"Oh…I could've sworn…"

Johnstone began to move and attempted to get up.

"Nathan, go help him."

Johnstone was physically sore from his ordeal and had a severe headache. He motioned with his hands that he was all right, considering what had happened.

"Oh…thank you, gentlemen," Johnstone said groggily, as he acknowledged their help. He looked over at the woman, and said, "I saw that woman with a man in this alley. I approached them and he attacked me."

"Where did he go?" Nathan asked.

"I don't know. I was knocked out."

The officers helped Johnstone stand. He was wobbly at first, but quickly gained his footing as his head cleared.

"Yes!" Johnstone exclaimed, as he remembered the vision. "I understand now!"

"Understand what, Sir?" Nathan asked.

Johnstone looked at the officers, "I don't think you'd understand if I told you, but I must take my leave now."

The officers were confused.

"I don't have time to explain. Have the constables take this woman to the police station so the investigators can question her. You two should go to Whitechapel and continue looking for the killer."

"Very well, Sir, but what about you?"

"I must leave, as I have a matter to attend to."

Johnstone walked as quickly as he could. He was in pain, but he put that aside as he had been trained to do. He made his way towards Marylebone Street, where he hired a cab. He instructed the coachman to drive as fast as he could to Thurrock.

** 8:30 P.M. (3) **

"How could it be him?" Violetta exclaimed.

"I don't know, but we totally missed this!"

Potter saw that Violetta was looking at the intruder. "Don't look at its eyes!" he instructed, as he grabbed her arm and positioned her behind him.

"I warned you," the intruder growled at Potter. "I saw you trying to interfere and then move in and take over after I was gone!"

"What do you mean 'move in'?"

"I wasn't even buried yet, and you were trying to make love to my wife!"

"Morrison, I was helping your family settle its affairs…"

"…and creating your own opportunities with my wife!" The color of his eyes turned a darker red.

"Morrison…"

The being ignored Potter and turned its attention to Violetta. "…and you, my dear. I stand here like this because of you! I was taken from life and all that I loved, and now I am not even permitted to die!"

"What do you want, Morrison?" Potter challenged.

"What do I want?" he grinned. "I want the two of you, of course!" Morrison stepped towards them.

The two instinctively moved backwards, away from Morrison's advance. However, they were quickly running out of space to retreat as they neared the wall by the couch.

"Potter, I shall make you like me. You will be my slave and do my bidding from now on." He smiled, and continued, "Violetta..."

Hearing her name called, she instinctively looked at Morrison and was immediately put under his control. As she was behind him, Potter was not aware that this had occurred.

"Yes, Violetta, that's it. I am going to make you my eternal love."

Potter realized now that something had happened and turned his head to look back at her.

"Damn you to hell, you bastard!" Potter yelled as he lunged at Morrison.

He knew that Morrison's transformation had given him considerable more strength than he had when he was alive. At best, he could only slow Morrison's advance while he tried to think of alternatives to save Violetta and himself.

"Violetta, run away!" Potter yelled hoping to break her out of the trance.

His words had no effect. Potter and Morrison twisted and turned in their struggle. Then, Morrison pushed Potter back into the couch.

"Violetta, run outside now!" Potter yelled as he fell backwards and lost his grip on Morrison.

With Potter sprawled on the couch, Morrison turned his attention to Violetta. He approached her, making sure to maintain his gaze on her and keep her eyes transfixed on his. She was standing in front of the couch. Morrison was in the middle of the room stepping towards her, with the desk directly behind him.

Seeing Morrison advancing the short distance to where Violetta stood, Potter frantically rolled himself off the couch. As he fell to the floor, he pushed Violetta. She likewise fell to the floor and was out of Morrison's reach for the moment. Potter continued to roll on the floor until he came in contact with Morrison. He wrapped his arms around Morrison's legs and pulled on them. Morrison lost his balance and fell backwards to the floor.

Potter stood and started towards Violetta to try to get her out of the cottage. Morrison gave a low growl as he rose from the floor. Seeing Morrison's movement, Potter changed his direction, lowered his head and, using his shoulder, slammed into Morrison's chest. Morrison fell backwards and landed on top of the desk. Potter jumped on top of Morrison.

The force of the impact of the two men on the desk caused it to shift and hit the wall. The loose dowel that held the sword fell out of its hole and dropped to the desk. The sword, no longer balanced in its position, also fell. It hit the desk, making a clanging noise, and then bounced to the floor. During the struggle, one of the men kicked the sword. It slid away from the desk and came to rest near the couch. The two were wrestling on the desk. Papers and books were moving and falling off the desk and onto the floor.

"Violetta," Potter yelled, "for God's sake, get up and run outside!"

Morrison's control over her was wearing off, and she was

becoming aware of the events in the room. She saw the two fighting on the desk and screamed.

"Run now! I can't hold him much longer!"

Violetta stood and started towards the door.

"No," Morrison shouted, "you two are mine!"

Morrison positioned himself so that he could push Potter off him. As he did so, Potter's arm struck the oil lamp that was on the desk. It crashed to the floor. As the glass oil well shattered, oil splattered and spread about the area. The flame quickly grew in size as it rode on the spreading oil. The papers and books lying on the floor provided kindling to enable the fire to hasten its growth. Oil also had splashed onto Potter's and Morrison's pants. It did not take long for the flames to find them. Potter screamed and Morrison howled as they felt the burning on their legs. Violetta ran to the door as the fire increased in its intensity.

"Mr. Potter," she called, "come on! We must go now!"

Potter's and Morrison's legs were now almost totally engulfed in flames. Potter was continuing his efforts to hold back Morrison so that Violetta could get safely out of the cottage, but she was indecisive and had not left. The flames were beginning to creep up the rest of their bodies.

Potter turned his head as best he could, and looked at Violetta, "Go now!" was his painfully spoken plea.

Morrison looked at Potter and growled. His incisors were elongated and ready. "I will take you with me!"

Morrison attempted to sink his teeth into Potter's neck. Potter tried to push away with one hand and hold off Morrison's head with the other. The fire on his legs, however, was beginning to incapacitate him.

Violetta started to leave as Potter had directed, but hearing Morrison's words made her stop. She quickly looked about the floor.

Potter was losing his battle with Morrison. Even though he also was burning, his strength and power were not waning as quickly as Potter's were. Just as Morrison's incisors were making contact with Potter's neck, the being suddenly screamed and let go of him.

Potter fell to the floor. He tried to crawl away from Morrison and the fire, but his legs were too badly burnt to permit him to move. Violetta was standing near Morrison. Potter saw that she was holding the sword and had cut open one of Morrison's arms. Morrison was almost covered in flames, but he growled and started towards her.

"No more nightmare!" she screamed as she held up the sword and swung it at Morrison.

The sword had been well maintained and the blade kept sharp. As the blade struck the side of Morrison's neck, it sliced through to the other side, severing his head from his body. The head rolled on the floor and stopped near the broken oil lamp, where it burst into flames. The rest of Morrison's body collapsed in a fiery heap on the floor.

Violetta, still holding the sword, quickly went over to Potter. She tried to find a place on his body that she could grab hold of in order to move him, but it was too late.

Potter looked at her one last time. "Please go now," he pleaded weakly as he died.

"You great man."

Crying, she ran outside to safety and turned to look at the cottage. Fire was now breaking out through the thatch roof. The heat, smoke and the burning embers were billowing towards her. She moved further away from the cottage to a place that was safer, at least for the moment.

She began to feel heat and a pain at her feet. Looking down, she saw that her dress had caught on fire. She ran to the water pump by the carriage house and doused the flames. With the layers of clothing she was wearing, she did not sustain more than minor burns on her legs. She dropped to her knees, buried her head in her hands and cried uncontrollably.

A chilly, light rain began to fall. As it hit the burning structure, the droplets made a sizzling sound on the burning wood. The precipitation, however, was insufficient in volume to have any real effect on the fire. The cottage was a total loss and burned to the ground.

** 11:00 P.M. **

Mary Jane was sitting at a small table at The Britannia Public House. She was in the company of a young, well dressed man with a well-groomed moustache. Both were very intoxicated. Needing to earn some money, Mary Jane asked the man if he wanted to go to her room. He finished his ale, politely declined her offer, stood and staggered out of the pub. Disappointed at the rejection, she ordered another pint of beer.

"Miss, may I offer you some of mine?"

She looked up at a short, stout man who was wearing a shabby, long overcoat and a billy cock hat. His blotchy face, with its small side-whiskers and thin moustache, was not attractive. However, Mary Jane noticed he was holding a full pail of beer. She smiled at him and motioned with her hands for him to sit. As soon as he put the pail on the table, Mary Jane dunked her mug into it. She pulled out the mug and drank half its contents in one swallow.

After some common small talk and another mug of beer, Mary Jane asked the inevitable question. This time she received a positive response to her offer. The two left the pub and walked to her room. He carried the pail of beer in one hand.

It was a chilly night. Mary Jane not only walked arm-in-arm with him to stay warm, but also to maintain physical contact to keep him interested along the way. When they stopped at a street corner, she would tighten her grip on him and reach up to give him a little peck on the cheek before they crossed the street.

Later, as midnight approached, a neighbor friend and fellow prostitute Mary Ann Cox came home to warm herself for a short while. She saw Mary Jane and the man standing outside of Mary Jane's room.

As Cox passed by, she greeted her friend, "It's a nasty night to be standing outside, Mary Jane! You'll catch your death of cold if you don't go in to warm yourself like I am!"

"Good night, Mary Ann," Mary Jane responded, as Cox walked by her. "I think tonight I am going to sing!"

Mary Jane gave the man another kiss on the cheek and bid him farewell. He walked away and Mary Jane went into her room. A few minutes later, she began to sing her favorite Irish lullaby, "A Violet from Mother's Grave." When intoxicated, she was known to sing this song repeatedly and very loudly during all hours of the night and early morning. Many times her singing disturbed her neighbors. Usually, to avoid a confrontation, the neighbors would let her sing without comment.

As she sang, she also cleaned herself and prepared to go back outside. As the midnight hour struck, Mary Jane took the money she had just earned and walked back to The Britannia Pub where she was able to purchase a meal of fish and potatoes.

XXVI.

(November 9)
** 1:00 A.M. **

The coachman left Johnstone at what used to be the front door to the cottage. The cold rain continued to make a sizzling sound as it struck the hot, burning wood in testament to the continued intensity of the fire. Steam rose in forms of ghostly figures of water vapor and smoke accompanied by an occasional "crack" and flying sparks that eerily danced in the night air. Most of the building was rubble as Johnstone surveyed what he could from the glow of orange embers and what fire continued to burn. He tried to speculate what had happened, but could arrive at no answers. He lived too far from the nearest town. No one would have noticed the fire and been able to summon a fire brigade to come to put out the blaze. He felt desolate and helpless amid the ruins of what once was his home.

He walked around the perimeter of the structure looking for any possible hint or clue. The night was too dark to give up any secrets. He walked to the carriage house, which still stood undamaged, and looked through a window. The carriage was still inside. He walked over to the stable, and in the stall he found his horse still there. His puzzlement grew, as he wondered why Potter had not taken the carriage to get help. Thinking that perhaps Potter had sought the safety of the carriage house, Johnstone went to the side of the building where there was a narrow side door. He opened it and went inside.

"Potter?"

There was no answer.

"Potter, are you in here?"

He heard what sounded like someone breathing heavily. There was no light, so he could not tell from where it came.

"Who's in here? Potter is that you?"

He heard movement again, which sounded like the braces of the carriage squeaking lightly. He moved closer to the carriage and heard whimpering coming from within. He opened one of the doors to the carriage. His action was immediately met with a loud scream. Then metal clanked wildly on both sides of the doorframe of the carriage. Not knowing what it was, he stepped back to maintain a safe distance. As he moved back, however, what was inside the carriage now leaned out the door and continued to scream and swing wildly with what it had in its hand.

"Go away! Leave me alone!"

"Violetta?"

There was no answer, but the screaming stopped.

"Violetta! It's Colonel Johnstone!"

"My Colonel?" was the quiet, weakened response.

"Yes, it's me."

She jumped out of the carriage and reached for Johnstone as if to hug him. Neither could see in the darkness, but Johnstone felt the sword touch his chest as Violetta neared him. He stepped back to protect himself, and then made a best guess and grabbed the arm that was holding the sword. She was still panicked from her ordeal and held tightly onto the sword.

"Violetta, I'm here. It's all right now. Please let go of the sword," he whispered gently to her. "Let go of the sword, before you hurt me."

Recognizing his voice, and realizing how close she had come to harming him, helped orient her to the present. She relaxed her grip enough to permit Johnstone to take the sword from her. He dropped it on the floor away from where she stood. Reaching to find him, Violetta wrapped her arms around him in a tight hug and resumed crying uncontrollably. Johnstone put his hands around her and rubbed her back gently, as he tried to calm her.

"Oh, Colonel," she continued to sob, "it terrible…Dear God, terrible what I do!"

"Violetta, whatever happened, it's over now. It's all right."

"The dead Colonel Morrison came back!"

"Yes, I know. I tried to get here as soon as I found out, but I was too late.

"He kill Mr. Potter."

"What?"

"He kill Mr. Potter. Then I kill him."

"You killed Colonel Morrison?"

"It wasn't him. It was man in river who come. It was monster. He try kill me. Mr. Potter save me. I try save him, but no time."

Johnstone could not comprehend what Violetta was telling him. He had no doubt, however, that the events she was describing had indeed happened. He felt himself weaken in the knees at the news of the loss of his trusted friend.

"Violetta, I must sit down," his voice was shaky.

"Carriage only place sit now."

"That's fine, but I must sit."

Johnstone helped her into the carriage and then climbed into it as well. Violetta was shivering from shock and from the damp, chilly air. Johnstone closed the door. They sat on the seat and tightly held on to each other. He was soon shivering as much as Violetta and for the same reasons.

** 2:00 A.M. **

The rain that had started to fall an hour earlier was beginning to come down harder. As the night wore on, the temperature continued to fall, causing a thick fog to appear in the chilly, humid air. The poor weather conditions chased most of the people from the streets, but there were still sufficient numbers walking about to keep the pubs and taverns busy.

George Hutchinson had just returned to the area after being out of town all day. He was walking on Commercial Street towards home. Walking quickly and holding his jacket against him to try to keep the weather from giving him a chill, he crossed Thrawl Street and observed a well-dressed man standing near a building. They nodded slightly to each other, but took no real notice.

A couple of blocks further, he saw a woman walking towards him. As she approached, he recognized her.

"Good morning, Mr. Hutchinson."

They both stopped on the sidewalk together. He quickly noticed that she was intoxicated, a condition in which he frequently saw her.

"Miss Kelly," he smiled and politely nodded, "how are you tonight?"

Mary Jane was one who liked to converse with people, but because of the inclement weather she cut the discussion short, and stated the reason for her hailing him. "Mr. Hutchinson, can you lend me six pence?"

He shook his head. "I can't. I'm sorry. I spent all my money going down to Ronford today."

Mary Jane was disappointed, but politely nodded to him and said, "Good morning to you then. I must go and find some money."

"Good morning, Miss Kelly."

Mary Jane then walked onward in the direction of Thrawl Street. He watched her as she walked away. He put one of his hands in his pants pocket and felt the coins there. He then turned, watched her as she walked away, and then decided to follow her. He stopped when he saw her meet the man whom he had passed just moments before. Hutchinson was close enough to see and hear their conversation. They faced away from him, so he was not noticed despite his proximity to their location. Still, he moved closer to one of the buildings to help avoid any possible detection, and to get some protection from the rain.

The man, who had his hat pulled down over his eyes, put his right hand on Mary Jane's shoulder after she greeted him. He made a quick comment to which they both laughed. He then took his hand off her shoulder, leaned over, and whispered something in her ear.

"All right," Mary Jane responded.

"You will be all right for what I have told you," the man replied in a foreign accent.

He briefly lifted his hat, whereupon Hutchinson thought he saw some sort of glistening coming from the man's eyes.

The man then put his right hand back on Mary Jane's shoulder and the two began to walk towards Dorset Street. Hutchinson noticed that the man was carrying a small parcel in his left hand. Not recognizing the man as someone who lived in the area, he continued to follow the couple, but maintained a discreet distance.

The two stopped and stood for a moment under a street lamp outside The Queen's Head Public House, where they chatted momentarily while standing in the rain.

"Would you like to go inside to get a nip to warm up before we continue to my room?" Mary Jane asked.

"No, I'm fine for now. Besides, I think there soon will be plenty of time for me to warm up."

"All right, Love," she sounded somewhat disappointed.

"Oh, did you want something to drink?"

"No, Love, it's all right. We're not far from my place."

They then crossed Commercial Street and walked down Dorsett Street, stopping just outside of Miller's Court. Hutchinson continued to follow, remaining in the shadows as best he could to avoid being seen.

The couple stopped and talked for several more minutes. He

grabbed hold of her somewhat roughly.

"No, Love. I know many of the girls will satisfy their men almost anywhere, but I'm just not comfortable like that. I prefer it to be in my room, if you don't mind."

It began to rain heavily, which was not unnoticed by her date.

"All right, my dear," Mary Jane said in response to the man's comment on the rain. "Come along. You will be comfortable. It will be better there for you. You'll see."

The man put his arms around her and she kissed him. Her face was wet from the rain, and she reached into her coat.

"Oh, I've lost my handkerchief," she said.

"Permit me," the man said as he produced a red handkerchief from his coat and gave it to her.

"Thank you, Love. That was very nice of you."

She patted the handkerchief on her cheeks and around her forehead.

"Lucky for you, Love, that you're wearing that hat. Helps keep the rain off your face."

He nodded, and the two then walked down to Miller's Court. Hutchinson remained where he was for a short time. When he could no longer see them, he left, resuming his walk home.

XXVII.

Mary Jane invited the man into her room. When they were inside, she shut the door and started to open her coat. The man came up to her from behind and helped her take off the coat.

"Thank you, Love," she smiled as she took the coat and hung it neatly on the back of one of the chairs by the window.

"The weather certainly has made a turn for the worse tonight," she smiled.

The man agreed.

"I hope your nice coat doesn't get ruined from the rain. It looks soaked."

He looked down at it. "It'll be fine."

She started towards the fireplace, "Well, I'm going to take off my boots. They are soaked from the rain," she giggled. "Why don't you put your things on the table by the bed and make yourself comfortable? I'm sure you want to get out of your wet clothes. I'll be right with you, Love."

Mary Jane sat on the chair that was facing the fireplace, and began unbuttoning her boots. While doing this she softly sang her favorite Irish song. The man put his package on the table as she suggested. He then took off his coat and placed it on the same chair with her coat. He returned to the table by the bed, quietly opened the box and removed an item from it. He closed the box, put his hat over it and sat on the bed where he watched her.

"In case you notice it, Love. It feels a little chilly in here, because I have a broken window", she commented. "I can take care of that and make things a little more comfortable for us."

Mary Jane finished removing her boots and placed them neatly by the fireplace. She put a couple of pieces of wood on the low-burning fire to warm the room, and then started towards the bed.

"Oh," she responded somewhat surprised, "I thought you would be ready for me."

He motioned for her to come closer to the bed. She did as requested, and stood before him. He put his hands on her hips and slowly turned her around. He stood behind her and began to unbutton her dress.

"Thank you, Love," she acknowledged his assistance. "You are certainly quite the gentleman!" she giggled again.

She removed her dress and walked over to the table by the window. She neatly folded the dress and placed it on the chair.

Now, just wearing a chemise and stockings, she turned to go back to the bed. "You know, Love, most men won't take the time to help a girl undress. They just want us to throw the dress up over us, do it and get on their way. It's nice to find a gentleman like you for a change."

The man closed his eyes and nodded to her. He then reopened his eyes and looked at her. For a second she thought she had seen something in his gaze, but discounted it as she returned to the bed.

The man, still clothed, was sitting at the head of the bed. Mary Jane knelt on the middle of the bed, and faced him.

"Now, Love," she stated as she put her hands on his thighs, "what can I do to make you comfortable?"

He motioned for her to turn around. She did as requested.

"You want me to take this off too?"

He knelt behind her and put his left hand on her left shoulder. He applied some pressure on it and started to massage her.

"Mmm," she closed her eyes, "that feels very good. Love, would you mind doing my other shoulder too?"

He applied more pressure on her left shoulder and his grip on her became stronger. She felt him as he pressed his chest against her back, and held her even tighter.

"Now, Love, don't hurt me," she tried to squirm.

He put his right arm on her hip, and ran it along her side, continuing up to her right shoulder. He continued moving his arm until his right hand was under her chin. Then, he made a sudden, swift motion across her neck with the implement he was holding.

"Oh, murder!" she cried, as she felt a sharp cutting pain as it started on the left side of her neck, dug in deeply and then quickly continued across to the right side.

Passersby, and neighbors who were in their rooms, heard Mary Jane's cry. However, such cries were commonplace in the East End, and usually received very little notice.

The killer hacked and sliced at Mary Jane with a maniacal ferociousness that was heretofore unseen in any of the previous murders. He opened her chest and removed her still beating heart. As she lay dead on the bed, her soft, lifeless eyes gazed towards him. Seeing her still pretty face incensed him even more. He took his knife and hacked away at her facial features, including gouging out her eyes. When he had finished his frenzied vivisection, no one looking upon the remains would ever have been able to tell that Mary Jane Kelly had been a beautiful woman. She was brutalized beyond recognition. Her sweet singing voice was silenced forever.

He cleaned himself and put on his coat and hat. He placed her heart in the case with his knife. The killer beast then left Mary Jane's apartment, taking his souvenir with him, and leaving her intestines in a pile on the table near the bed.

XXVIII.

The morning was cold and heavily overcast, but at least the rain had stopped. Violetta and Johnstone, still clinging to each other, had fallen asleep in the carriage. The horse had awakened in its stable and its movement roused its owner. As he awoke, he looked at Violetta. There was a slight, peaceful smile on her face. He thought how beautiful she looked as she slept, and he felt warmness in his heart for her.

Johnstone attempted to get out of the carriage as quietly as possible so that he could tend to the horse. He did not want to wake Violetta. However, the carriage rocked and squeaked as he exited and shut the door. He looked through the window and saw that she was still asleep. He bent over and picked up his sword from the floor, left the carriage house and went to the stable.

He put hay in the horse's feeding trough and made sure that there was sufficient water in the water tray. He then walked over to the ruins of what used to be his home. The heavy rainfall during the night had extinguished almost all of the fire. There were just a couple of hot spots remaining where some small wisps of smoke were rising upwards from the orange glowing embers within the gray ashes. The daylight revealed to him what the night concealed, but the truth he had already known. There was nothing left.

He walked into what used to be the front room. On the floor near the debris of what was once his desk, he recognized the remains of Potter and Morrison. The intensity of the flames and the heat of the fire had turned their bodies to ashes. However, the ashes were arranged such that he could see the men's physical outlines and ascertain that they had been in a mortal struggle. The sight made him weak in the knees and he started to become emotional, but he fought back the feeling.

"What you do now?"

Johnstone jumped, startled by the unexpected voice, and turned around. Violetta was standing outside the remains of the cottage.

"I don't know," he said lowly, as he shook his head. "I have lost just about everything that I have cared for, except you."

She blushed, but was unable to smile.

"It sad day. Even weather know it sad day."

Violetta watched as Johnstone dropped the sword and went into the carriage house. He came out carrying a bucket and shovel. He returned to the area where his friends laid, and put their remains in the bucket. Johnstone then went to the area that had been his bedroom. With the remains now cleared from the floor, Violetta entered the cottage area and joined him. He found a good-sized piece of bedding that had survived the fire, picked it up and tore off the burnt edges. He carried the bedding to the front room area and picked up the bucket. He handed the bedding to Violetta and asked her to carry it so that he could pick up his sword. The two walked to the river. Neither said a word.

Johnstone stepped onto the rock ledge, putting the items he was carrying on the rock. He took the bedding from Violetta and spread it flat. Picking up the bucket, he gently poured the ashes of his comrades into a pile in the middle of the material. The ashes were wet from the rain and melded together like a paste. He took the edges of the fabric and folded them to enclose the ashes. He twisted the ends together to form a ball, and asked Violetta to hold it closed. She hesitated at first, but did it for him. He took the sword and used the blade to thread all of the edges to hold the bedding together. He picked it up and stood close to the water. He looked back at Violetta. He felt a couple of tears roll down his face. Violetta was solemn, but did not cry.

"Neither man asked for, or deserved this," he told her.

She nodded.

"They were just trying to help people."

Johnstone looked out upon the river and then threw the bedding as far as he could onto the water. It landed with a light splash and floated, slowly drifting away with the current. Violetta joined him on the rock ledge.

"Farewell, old friends," he said, as he stood and saluted them.

Potter's and Morrison's final journey was short-lived, and Johnstone and Violetta watched as the bedding material slowly absorbed the water. With the sword acting as a weight, the bundle sank from view.

Johnstone looked at Violetta and took hold of one hand. "What are you going to do?" he asked her.

"I know not. I must think what comes next now."

"What is there for you to do besides go back to what you were?"

"I could go to West End. There are houses there. Some say I do good there, because I pretty. More money on West End. Maybe I take good care of daughter now. I can start new there."

He grunted slightly, "Returning to do what you were doing before is not starting new."

"I have work. Need take care of little girl and mother. No work, we don't eat."

"Some work," Johnstone replied. "Is that really a way to live?" He shrugged, and then concluded, "I guess in a way that is better than the nothing that I now have."

He let go of her hand, and they turned to walk off the ledge and back onto the field. As she started, Violetta stepped on a small box.

"What this?" she asked as she bent over, picked it up and handed it to Johnstone. "It fall out bedding?"

He took it in his hands. He was not aware when he threw the ashes into the river that the small jewel case had fallen from his jacket and landed on the rock ledge.

"No," he replied, "it didn't fall out of there."

He opened it and showed it to her.

"It beautiful."

"I got it for you to show you that you have become a part of me, and live in my heart."

She looked at him, "I…"

"May I put it on you?"

"I not…"

"Please? It would make me very happy if you would wear it and remember me."

"I never forget you, or your friends. You are all great men. You so kind and good to me. You my great friend."

"I will always be your friend, or more, if that is what you want, and will let me become."

She turned and opened her collar as Johnstone put the chain around her neck. She put her hand on the heart pendant, and her eyes became teary.

"I wear always for you."

They were looking at the river once more. The breeze was chilled as it came off the cold water. A light mist rose from the river. Johnstone closed his coat against the cold. Violetta did likewise as she stood silently alongside him. She pressed her hand into her coat until she felt the heart pendant. She clutched it from outside her coat and held onto it. They stood and continued to gaze upon the water. Watching the slow current and hearing the waves gently rapping against the shore was hypnotizing. Both were saddened over the events of the previous night, and they struggled within their own minds and thoughts over what to do next and how to resume their individual lives.

XXIX.

Regular East End activity on this late Friday morning had already commenced. It was not until almost seven hours following the brutal slaying of Mary Jane that a rent collector discovered her remains. As the police converged on Miller's Court off Dorset Street, news of the murder began to spread throughout the district. The relaxed attitude regarding the Ripper killings that had returned to the district quickly vanished. It had been one month since the double event. Now, a renewed concern and panic began to permeate through the East End once more.

At this time, a young woman was at her usual street corner where she sold roasted chestnuts. The side street was narrow, and was about a two-minute walk from Miller's Court.

She sold a handful of chestnuts to a ragged, old man. It would probably be his only meal for the day. As the old man left, another stepped up to her. He was well dressed, wearing a top hat and long coat, and was carrying a small, shiny black bag.

"Good day, Sir. Would you like to buy some chestnuts? Only two pence a handful."

He shook his head.

"Oh," she was disappointed, "then what can I do for you, Sir?"

"I suppose," he softly replied, so that only she could hear him, "you have heard about the murder in Dorset Street?"

"Oh, yes, Sir, I have. It's horrible!"

The man grinned and responded, "I know more about it than you."

He then stared into her face in an almost trance-like manner. After just a few seconds, he broke his gaze and ran down an adjacent narrow street. When he was two blocks away, he stopped, turned and looked back at the street seller. She had been watching him. He suddenly looked up, then turned the corner and vanished. She continued to watch to see if he would come back in view. A blue fog gathered at the location where she last saw him, and drifted from sight as it moved down the side street.

On dark, overcast days following a night of rain, fog was a common occurrence, especially on chilly, humid days. The blue fog easily blended with the gray fog and the daily smog that clung to the East End. It drifted silently, purposely towards the docks and the river.

St. Katherine's Dock, located adjacent to the Tower Bridge and the Tower of London, had been constructed over a half-century before. It was an artificial basin and waterway lined with carved stone and concrete walls that led to a passageway to and from the Thames. Most of the area where the ships moored was surrounded by large warehouses. One such building contained a clock tower with an open ground floor. The open area permitted incoming and outgoing cargo to be easily staged and worked. A large number of granite pillars were located throughout the ground floor. These gave support to the four floors above.

For a midday Friday, the dock was extraordinarily quiet. Less than half the berths had ships docked, and little movement of cargo going onto or off the ships was occurring.

The fog moved into the dock area. It had a slight blue tint to it, and was elongated with an extension protruding from each side of its mid-section. The protrusions waved slightly up and down as the fog moved towards the warehouse with the clock tower. It was moving slightly behind a well-dressed man who was running towards the warehouse. Now and then, the fog came in contact with him, and administered a small electrical discharge. The man jumped from the shock, and then waved his arms as if trying to fan the fog away from him.

The man ran into the cargo staging area of the warehouse and stopped. He looked back and saw that the fog had slowed its approach and reshaped itself to fit into the narrower space. He ran deeper into the staging area and ducked behind one of the pillars. He peeked from around it and saw the fog enter the staging area and continue to move towards him.

During the day, even though heavy cloud cover obscured the sunlight, the light that did get through was sufficient to weaken the fog's strength. However, now that it had entered a much darker area, its strength was significantly, but not totally, revived as evident by the brighter blue hue to its structure.

The fog was now growing in density and shrinking in size, and it continued approaching the man. He stood behind the pillar, remaining out of sight of the fog. Opening the small bag he was carrying, he removed a long, thin knife with a razor-sharp edge, and held it in his right hand.

The fog moved around the pillar and came in contact with the man. It kept coming until it had completely engulfed him. The fog produced more electrical discharges that were inflicted on its prey.

The man slashed wildly with the knife at the fog in response. His actions had no effect. The fog began to revolve around him. The man started to turn with the motion, but continued to slash with the knife. From the combination of turning with the fog and the accompanying electrical discharges, the man dizzied, soon lost his balance and fell to the floor.

The fog quickly moved away and coalesced into the being that had been stalking him. The man quickly stood and, holding the knife, assumed a defensive posture. He was still dizzy from being repetitively turned around, and swayed as he stood.

"I know who you are," the man remarked.

"And I know what you are," the being growled, as he began to approach the man.

The man continued to slash wildly through the air with the knife. Undaunted, the being continued to close in. At one point, the tip of the knife cut the being's cheek.

The man laughed maniacally, "My blade is still sharp. My work is not yet done!"

The being's cheek bled slightly, and then quickly healed itself. There was no mark or scar left to show that there had ever been an injury.

The being's red eyes glared at the man. "You're time here is done! I shall return you to the hell where you belong!"

The man lunged forward with the knife pointing at the being. It plunged through the being's coat and into its abdomen. As the knife was pulled out, the being grabbed the man's hand and tightly held it in place. The man struggled, but was unable to break the grip and get away. The new wound that was inflicted by the knife, as happened with the cut on the cheek, quickly healed itself.

The being twisted the man's hand to the point that the sound of bones breaking, and the man's screaming from the resulting pain, echoed through the area. With a broken hand, the man was no longer able to hold onto the knife. It fell to the concrete floor, and the metallic clanking from the blade likewise sounded through the area.

The being pulled the man closer to him and held onto his arm. Its red eyes were searing in rage as he growled, "If you know who I am, then you know my purpose here. It shall be completed now. You can no longer cause distractions by using letters to give false information, or wrongly lead people to chase me instead of you!"

The man laughed and looked directly into the being's eyes, "Are you going to make me like you? Go ahead! Do it! Then my knife will be forever sharp, and I will continue to rip the unsuspecting. I will continue like this forever!"

The being now twisted the man's arm. More bones shattered from the continued pressure. "That is not to be your fate," the being clarified.

The man laughed through his pain, "You cannot do anything to me that will stop me! Yes, you can terminate me now, but I will come back time and time again. You don't have that control over me! I will always have my sharp knife with me!"

"Perhaps, but for you, your time of terror at this moment is ended."

The man was held in such a way that his head was turned, and he was unable to see that the fingernail on the being's right index finger had grown long and sharp. The being held the man at arm's length and raised his right arm. In a swift right-to-left motion across the man's neck, the being sliced the neck open in the same manner in which the man had sliced open his victims.

Blood spurted from the gaping wound. The being let the blood fall to the warehouse floor. It had no desire to ingest it. As the blood drained from his body, the man's face lost its color. He grew weaker as his heart pounded harder, trying to fill its chambers with the blood that was no longer there.

The being released his hold on the man, who staggered away, and laughed defiantly, "You may have ended this now, but I will soon return!"

The man then fell to the floor and died.

"I think not," the being remarked, and spat on the body.

The saliva acted as an acid and quickly spread. The body began to bubble and sizzle. A small plume of smoke rose from the corpse carrying with it the smell of dead, burning flesh. The being went over to the small bag that the man had been carrying and opened it. He put his hand into it and removed the heart. He summoned some saliva from his mouth and gently put it on the heart. The acid in the saliva began to dissolve it, as the being held it in his hands. He watched as the heart grew smaller. At one point, he thought he heard the sound of a woman softly singing an Irish ballad. The sweet tone of the voice brought tears of blood that rolled from his eyes and down his cheeks. Then, the heart was gone, and the song ended.

He looked back at the corpse and saw that it, too, had dissolved and left no trace. The being transformed itself into a blue fog, and drifted out of the warehouse staging area. It moved over the dock and gently drifted to the Thames, where it moved down the river towards Thurrock.

XXX.

Johnstone and Violetta had returned to the burned-out remains of the cottage. Johnstone took one last look to see if there was anything that might have survived the fire. Nothing useful was found.

The temperature turned colder as the day wore on. Johnstone suggested that it was time for him to take Violetta home. He hitched his horse to the carriage, and prepared for the journey to Whitechapel. When he was ready, he found Violetta standing in the field, midway to the river. He walked over to her.

"It shame," she said. "You beautiful house. What can you do now? Build new home?"

Johnstone took a deep breath and shook his head. "No," he replied, "I think not."

"What you do then?"

"I was thinking perhaps I will start over again, but not by rebuilding here. After what I've seen, I no longer have the desire to live here. I want to start over by going somewhere new to live, truly starting over from nothing, to build a new life."

"Where you go?"

"I have a distant cousin who lives in a small town in America. It is north of New York City."

"America? That long way."

"Yes it is. I visited him many years ago. It is pretty there, with the river and mountains. Even the name of the town he lives in is different."

"What is that?"

"Poughkeepsie."

"Pou…I cannot say name."

"Poughkeepsie," Johnstone repeated, as he smiled faintly. "Doesn't matter. Not much matters now."

"But it different and new life for you, right?"

"Yes."

"Happy life?"

"I hope so. It depends how I make it."

"You deserve happy life. I want you be happy."

They stood together in silence for a moment.

"It's getting colder, Violetta. We should be leaving now. There is nothing left here."

Johnstone turned and started walking to the carriage.

"My Colonel, look at river!"

Johnstone stopped and turned. Violetta was pointing at a fog bank drifting above the water. She became agitated as she recognized a blue hue to the fog. Johnstone rejoined her. The fog began to swirl and move towards the shore. As it approached, it elongated and exhibited an extremity on each side of its mid-section.

"It comes for us!" Violetta cried in alarm. "We must run! Quick!"

"There's no place to hide from this. There's no time to run."

The fog approached them as they stood in the field. Johnstone put his arms around Violetta to keep her from running. She struggled slightly, but stopped as the fog made contact.

"We die now, too," she said.

The fog came upon them, and rotated around them as they felt it. They smelled its lavender fragrance, were rendered unconscious, and fell to the ground. It hovered and remained with them for several minutes. Then, it began to rise, elongated itself and, with its extremities, made a flying motion as it went higher in the sky. The two awoke moments after the fog broke its physical contact with them.

"Look!" Violetta exclaimed, as they stood. "The fog look like dove flying!"

"We'll be all right now."

"Yes, I understood. I felt it. It told me so."

They watched as it continued to climb higher in the sky. It intermixed with the gray clouds and, as it did so, produced blue flashes of light. Then it was gone.

"It strange, but beautiful," Violetta said.

"We must leave now."

"All right. Yes."

They started towards the carriage. A moment later, they noticed that it had started to snow. First a few flakes were noticeable, and then a heavy flurry filled the air. They passed the remnants of the cottage and saw that the snow was beginning to cover the charred remains.

"Winter start now," Violetta observed. "Seasons have new beginning, too."

Johnstone opened the carriage door and started to help Violetta into the carriage. She started up the steps, but stopped. She looked out upon the ruins, the field and the river.

"What's wrong?" Johnstone asked.

"William, can child and mother also go to this how you say, 'Poughkeepsie', and start new life?"

Her question caught him off guard, and he could not respond.

"I think everyone, like everything here, need new start," she continued. "I love you, William. It truth, and I need you. It no new beginning for us if we not together."

She stepped down from the carriage and the two embraced. Johnstone, who had maintained his stoic manners throughout the tribulations of the past months, could no longer contain himself. He began to weep, and was comforted by Violetta.

Out of the entrails of evil, terror and death, the seed of love was planted, and had now sprouted to grow in good, peace and life.

Epilogue

"A Violet from Mother's Grave"

Scenes of my childhood arise before my gaze,
Bringing recollections of by-gone happy days,
When down in the meadows in childhood I would roam,
No one's left to cheer me now within that good old home;
Father and Mother they have passed away,
Sister and brother now lay beneath the clay,
But while life does remain to cheer me I'll retain,
This small violet I plucked from mother's grave.

Only a violet I plucked when but a boy,
And oftimes when I'm sad at heart
This flow'r has giv'n me joy;
But while life does remain, in memoriam I'll retain,
This small violet I plucked from mother's grave.

Well I remember my dear old mother's smile,
As she used to greet me when I returned from toil
Always knitting in the old arm chair.
Father used to sit and read for all the children there,
But now all is silent around the good old home,
They have all left me in sorrow for to roam.

But while life does remain, in memoriam I'll retain,
This small violet I plucked from mother's grave.

Only a violet I plucked when but a boy,
And oftimes when I'm sad at heart
This flow'r has giv'n me joy;
But while life does remain, in memoriam I'll retain,
This small violet I plucked from mother's grave.

- William H. Fox (1881)

Addendum

This work is dedicated to the memory of The Canonical Five: Mary Ann Nichols, Annie Chapman, Elizabeth Stride, Catherine Eddowes, and Mary Jane Kelly. They lived in extremely hard times. Their lives were difficult, as they tried to survive as best as they could. They did not deserve to have their days ended in the manner as fate had ordained for them. May you rest in peace.